Tinkercad Black Book

By
Gaurav Verma
(CADCAMCAE Works)

Edited by
Kristen

ISBN # 978-1-77459-146-8

NOTICE TO THE READER

DEDICATION

To teachers, who make it possible to disseminate knowledge
to enlighten the young and curious minds
of our future generations

To students, who are the future of the world

THANKS

To my friends and colleagues

To my family for their love and support

Training and Consultant Services

At CADCAMCAE WORKS, we provide effective and affordable one to one online training on various software packages in Computer Aided Design(CAD), Computer Aided Manufacturing(CAM), Computer Aided Engineering (CAE), Computer programming languages(C/C++, Java, .NET, Android, Javascript, HTML and so on). The training is delivered through remote access to your system and voice chat via Internet at any time, any place, and at any pace to individuals, groups, students of colleges/universities, and CAD/CAM/CAE training centers. The main features of this program are:

Training as per your need

Highly experienced Engineers and Technician conduct the classes on the software applications used in the industries. The methodology adopted to teach the software is totally practical based, so that the learner can adapt to the design and development industries in almost no time. The efforts are to make the training process cost effective and time saving while you have the comfort of your time and place, thereby relieving you from the hassles of traveling to training centers or rearranging your time table.

Software Packages on which we provide
basic and advanced training are:

CAD/CAM/CAE: CATIA, Creo Parametric, Creo Direct, SolidWorks, Autodesk Inventor, Solid Edge, UG NX, AutoCAD, AutoCAD LT, EdgeCAM, MasterCAM, SolidCAM, DelCAM, BOBCAM, UG NX Manufacturing, UG Mold Wizard, UG Progressive Die, UG Die Design, SolidWorks Mold, Creo Manufacturing, Creo Expert Machinist, NX Nastran, Hypermesh, SolidWorks Simulation, Autodesk Simulation Mechanical, Creo Simulate, Gambit, ANSYS and many others.

Computer Programming Languages: C++, VB.NET, HTML, Android, Javascript and so on.

Game Designing: Unity.

Civil Engineering: AutoCAD MEP, Revit Structure, Revit Architecture, AutoCAD Map 3D and so on.

We also provide consultant services for Design and development on the above mentioned software packages

For more information you can mail us at:
cadcamcaeworks@gmail.com

Table of Contents

Chapter 2 : Code Blocks

Chapter 3 : Circuits

Chapter 4 : Basics of Programming Code

Preface

Tinkercad is a free to use web based software provided by Autodesk. The software is very intuitive and provides tools to apply creativity in 3D designs. The application has three different workspaces 3D Design, Codeblocks, and Circuits. You can use drag and drop shapes to create simple as well as complex designs in 3D Design workspace. You can use visual programming codeblocks to create 3D shapes with the power of mathematical and logical formulas. You can create and simulation electrical/electronic circuits using the Circuits workspace. The software allows collaborations and educational setup naturally with perfectly coordinated tools.

The **Tinkercad Black Book**, 1st edition is written to help beginners in creating 3D designs, performing codeblock programming, and running advanced circuit simulations. The book covers all the workspaces of the application with great details on practical applications. The book follows a step by step methodology. In this book, we have tried to give real-world examples with real challenges of designing. The book covers almost all the information required by a learner to master the Tinkercad. Some of the salient features of this book are:

In-Depth explanation of concepts

Every new topic of this book starts with the explanation of the basic concepts. In this way, the user becomes capable of relating the things with real world.

Topics Covered

Every chapter starts with a list of topics being covered in that chapter. In this way, the user can easily find the topics of his/her interest easily.

Instruction through illustration

The instructions to perform any action are provided by maximum number of illustrations so that the user can perform the actions discussed in the book easily and effectively. There are about 400 illustrations that make the learning process effective.

Tutorial point of view

At the end of concept's explanation, the tutorial make the understanding of users long lasting. Almost each chapter of the book has tutorials that are real world projects. Moreover most of the tools in this book are discussed in the form of tutorials.

Formatting Conventions Used in the Text

All the key terms like name of button, tool, drop-down etc. are kept bold.

Free Resources

Link to the resources used in this book are provided to the users via email. To get the resources, mail us at ***cadcamcaeworks@gmail.com*** with your contact information. With your contact record with us, you will be provided latest updates and informations regarding various technologies. The format to write us mail for resources is as follows:

Subject of E-mail as ***Application for resources of .... book***.
Also, given your information like
Name:
Course pursuing/Profession:
Contact Address:
E-mail ID:

Note: We respect your privacy and value it. If you do not want to give your personal informations then you can ask for resources without giving your information.

About Authors

The author of this book, Gaurav Verma, has written and assisted in more than 17 titles in CAD/CAM/CAE which are already available in market. He has authored Autodesk Fusion 360 Black Book, AutoCAD Electrical Black Book, Autodesk Revit Black Books, and so on. He has provided consultant services to many industries in US, Greece, Canada, and UK. He has assisted in preparing many Government aided skill development programs. He has been speaker for Autodesk University, Russia 2014. He has assisted in preparing AutoCAD Electrical course for Autodesk Design Academy. He has worked on Sheetmetal, Forging, Machining, and Casting designs in Design and Development departments of various manufacturing firms. If you have any query/doubt in any CAD/CAM/CAE package, then you can contact the author by writing at cadcamcaeworks@gmail.com

For Any query or suggestion

If you have any query or suggestion, please let us know by mailing us on *cadcamcaeworks@gmail.com*. Your valuable constructive suggestions will be incorporated in our books and your name will be addressed in special thanks area of our books on your confirmation.

Chapter 1

Starting with Tinkercad

Topics Covered

The major topics covered in this chapter are:

- *Introduction to Tinkercad*
- *Starting with Tinkercad*
- *Starting a 3D Design*
- *Basic Shape Tools*
- *Design Starter Tools*
- *Creature and Character, Vehicles & Machines, Structures & Scenery, and Electronics Tools*
- *Fun & Games, Everyday Objects, Featured Collections, and Sim Lab Tools*
- *Shape Generator Tools*
- *Blocks Workspace*
- *Bricks Workspace*

INTRODUCTION

Tinkercad is an easy to use, browser-based 3D design tool. Tinkercad is used to build all types of creations by adding and removing shapes from the design workspace. Tinkercad is a free-of-charge, online 3D modeling program that runs in a web browser. Since it became available in 2011, it has become a popular platform for creating models for 3D printing as well as an entry-level introduction to constructive solid geometry in schools.

STARTING TINKERCAD

- To start **Tinkercad** in **Windows 10**, search for **Tinkercad** in any browser, the search results related to **Tinkercad** will be displayed; refer to Figure-1.

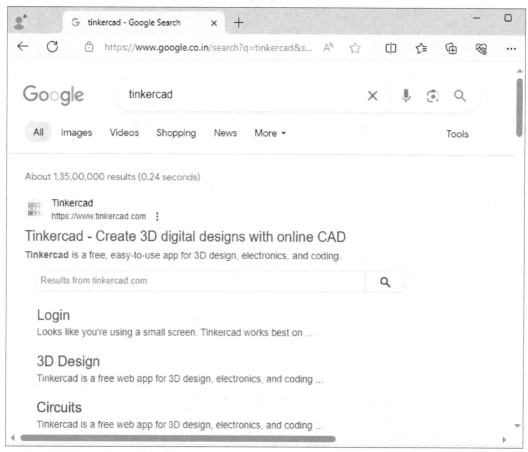

Figure-1. Tinkercad appearance browser

- Click on the first option from the search results displayed. Alternatively, you can open the link *www.tinkercad.com* in your web browser. The **Tinkercad** interface will be displayed; refer to Figure-2.

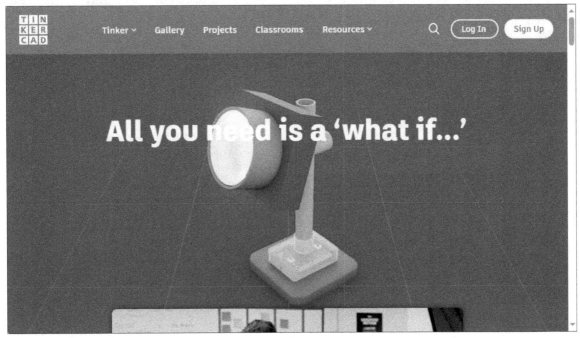

Figure-2. Tinkercad interface

Signing Up as Educator

- Click on the **Sign Up** button from the upper right corner of the page, the **Sign Up** page will be displayed; refer to Figure-3.

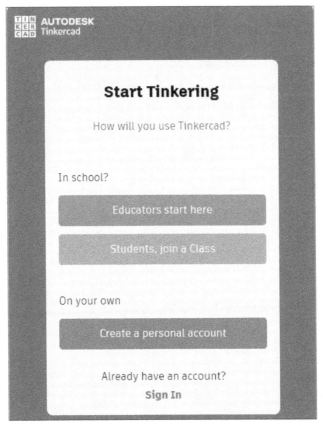

Figure-3. Sign Up page

- If you are an Educator or Trainer then click on the **Educators start here** button, the **Student safety and moderation** page will be displayed; refer to Figure-4.

- Click on the **Continue to start making my educator account**, the **Teacher Agreement** page will be displayed; refer to Figure-5.

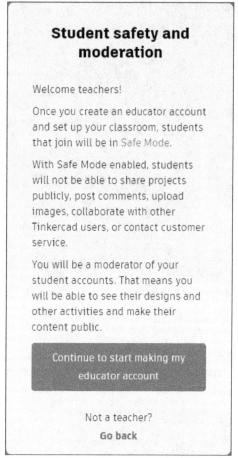

Figure-5. Teacher Agreement page

Figure-4. Student safety and moderation page

- Select the check box and click on the **I agree** button, the **Teacher Account** page will be displayed; refer to Figure-6.

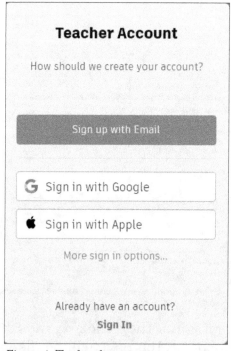

Figure-6. Teacher Account page

- Click on desired option and sign up by entering the required details or click on the **Sign In** button to join the tinkercad by entering the existing account details.
- If you want to invite students in the class then you can share your class link or class code to join them directly in the class. For this, click on the **Create new class** button from **Classes** section in your **Profile**; refer to Figure-7. The **Create new class** dialog box will be displayed; refer to Figure-8.

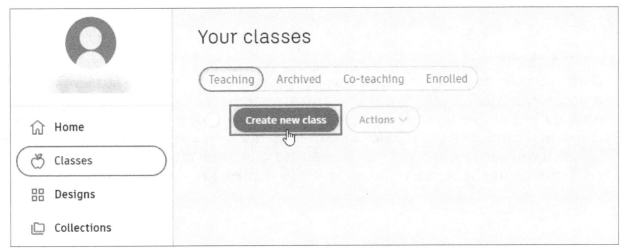

Figure-7. Create new class button

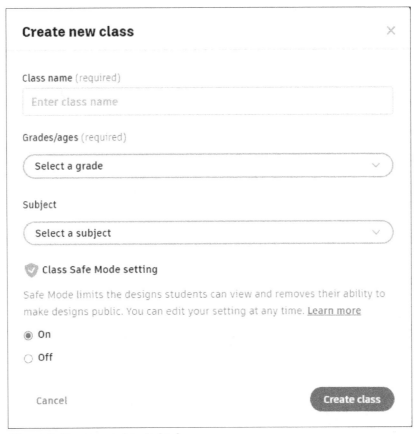

Figure-8. Create new class dialog box

- Specify required parameters in the dialog box and click on the **Create class** button. The class will be created with the name you specified in the **Class name** edit box; refer to Figure-9.

Figure-9. Class created

- Now, you can share the class link to your students or you can add students to your class by entering names of your students, they entered in their **Tinkercad** profile. After adding students, their name will appear in the page; refer to Figure-10. You can visit and modify the profile of your students by clicking on their table in the list. You can click on the **...** button from **Menu** column and award badges to your students using the shortcut menu; refer to Figure-11.

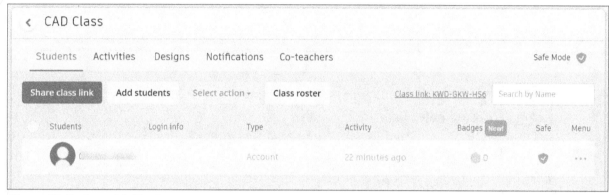

Figure-10. Student added in class

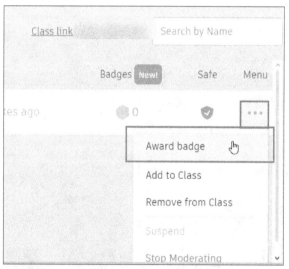

Figure-11. Award badge option

- After adding the students, click on the **Create your first activity** button from **Activities** tab of the class created; refer to Figure-12. The **New Activity** page will be displayed; refer to Figure-13.

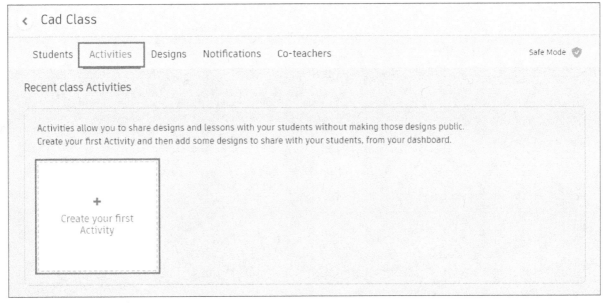

Figure-12. Activities tab

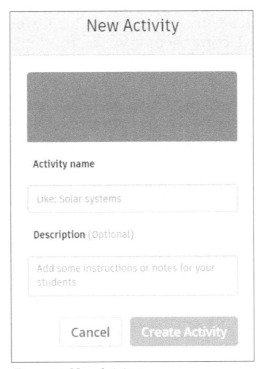

Figure-13. New Activity page

- Specify desired name and description of the activity in respective edit boxes and click on the **Create Activity** button. The activity will be created.
- Click on the created activity, the options related to the activity will be displayed; refer to Figure-14.

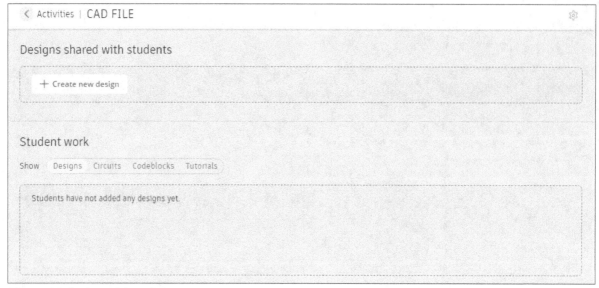

Figure-14. Options of the activity

- Click on the **+ Create new design** button and select desired workspace to work with. On creating desired design, your students will be able to see this design.
- As an educator, you will be able to check and modify designs created by students in your classroom by selecting them from the Student work area of the Activities page; refer to Figure-14.

Signing Up as Student

- If you are a student then click on the **Students, join a Class** button on **Sign Up** page of **Tinkercad**. The **Join Class** page will be displayed; refer to Figure-15.

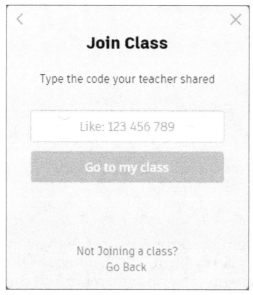

Figure-15. Join Class page

- Type the code in the box shared by your teacher and click on the **Go to my class** button. The **Sign in** page will be displayed.
- Sign in with your existing Tinkercad details. The class and activities created by the teacher will be displayed.
- Click on desired activity and start Tinkering. Your teacher will be able to check and modify your designs if needed.

Signing Up as Personal Account

- If you want to create a personal account then click on the **Create a personal account** and sign up with the required details or sign in with the existing details.
- If you already have an account on Tinkercad then click on the **Sign In** button from the dialog box.

After you have performed the above steps, the **Tinkercad** application window will be displayed; refer to Figure-16.

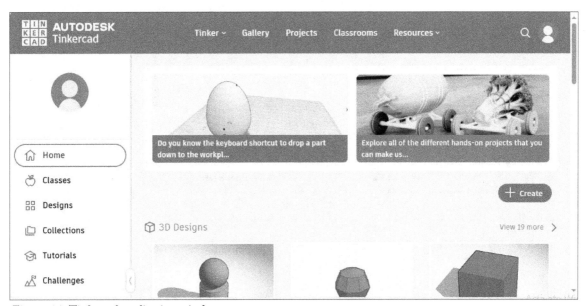

Figure-16. Tinkercad application window

Keyboard Shortcuts

AUTODESK Tinkercad — Keyboard shortcuts — Ctrl = Command   Alt = Option

Viewing 3D space

Fit selection into view	F
Orbit	Right mouse or Ctrl + Left mouse
Pan	Middle mouse or Shift + Right mouse
Zoom in or out	+ and - or Scroll

Shape properties

Group	Ctrl + G
Ungroup	Ctrl + Shift + G
Make a Hole	H
Make a Solid Color	S
Make Transparent	T
Lock or Unlock	Ctrl + L
Hide	Ctrl + H
Show all	Ctrl + Shift + H

Helpers

Place Ruler	R
Place Workplane	W
Place Workplane at shape	Shift + W
Show Shape Workplane	E

Move, rotate, and scale shapes

Rotate snap to 45°	Shift + Rotate handle
Scale about center	Alt + Scale handle
Uniform scale	Shift + Scale handle
Move 1 grid space (X/Y axis)	Arrows
Move up (Z axis)	Ctrl + Arrows up/down
Cruise tool	C

Commands

Copy	Ctrl + C
Paste	Ctrl + V
Duplicate, repeat Duplicate	Ctrl + D
Drag a copy	Alt + move shape
Undo last action	Ctrl + Z
Redo last action	Ctrl + Y
Select all	Ctrl + A
Select multiple	Shift
Drop to workplane	D
Align	L
Mirror or flip	M

STARTING 3D DESIGN

• Click on the **+Create** button from the application window, the three options will be displayed; refer to Figure-17. Click on the **3D Design** button, the 3D Design workspace will be displayed; refer to Figure-18.

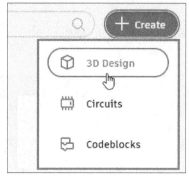

Figure-17. Create options

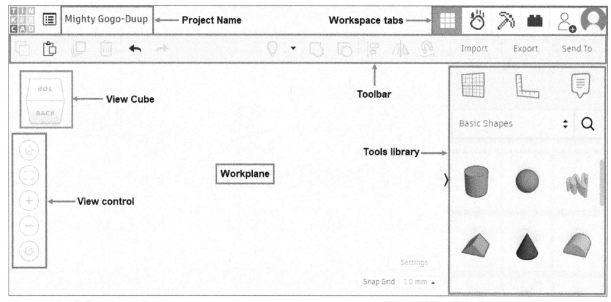

Figure-18. 3D Design workspace

Project Name

To modify the name of project, click on the project name and enter desired name in the box.

Toolbar

Toolbar is an important part of the user interface, providing easy access to the tools to design 3D models, circuits, or code. The procedure to use these tools are discussed next.

Creating Copy of Objects

The **Copy** tool is used to create copy of a shape in your design. The procedure to use this tool is discussed next.

• By default, the **Copy** tool is inactive. To activate the **Copy** tool, select the object in the workplane to be copied, the **Copy** tool will be activated.

- Click on the **Copy** tool from toolbar; refer to Figure-19. You can also create a copy by using keyboard shortcut **CTRL+C**. The object will be copied in clipboard (temporary memory of software).

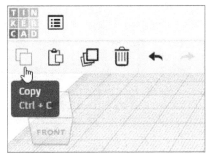

Figure-19. Copy tool

- Click on the **Paste** tool from toolbar. The copy of selected object will be created; refer to Figure-20. To create multiple copies, keep clicking the **Paste** button.

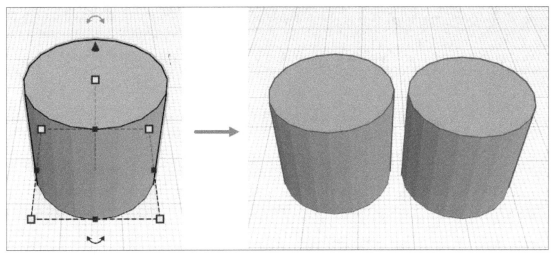

Figure-20. Object copied

Duplicate and repeat

The **Duplicate and repeat** tool is used to create place duplicate copy of selected object at the same location where original object is located. The procedure to use this tool is discussed next.

- Select the shape in the workplane to be duplicated and click on the **Duplicate and repeat** tool from toolbar; refer to Figure-21. The new shape will be duplicated on the selected shape.

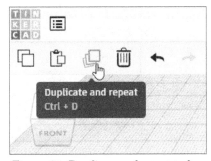

Figure-21. Duplicate and repeat tool

- Click and drag the shape to separate it from original shape; refer to Figure-22.

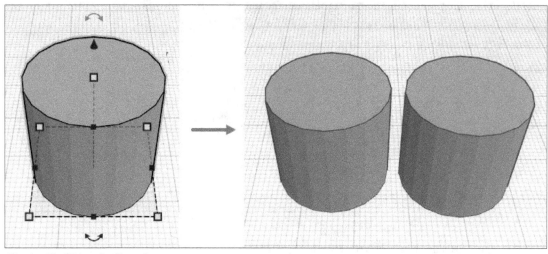

Figure-22. Object duplicated

- Once a duplicated shape has been placed, you can move or modify the duplicated shape. Click on the **Duplicate and repeat** tool again to create another duplicate copy with the changes applied.
- Continue clicking the **Duplicate and repeat** tool to create a pattern with the duplicates.

Undo tool

The **Undo** tool is used to reverse the last action in the design process of the model. The procedure to use this tool is discussed next.

- Click on the **Undo** tool from the toolbar; refer to Figure-23. You can also do this action by using keyboard shortcut **CTRL+Z**.

Figure-23. Undo tool

Redo tool

The **Redo** tool is used to reverse the recent undo action in the design process of the model. The procedure to use this tool is discussed next.

- Click on the **Redo** tool from the toolbar; refer to Figure-24. You can also do this action by using keyboard shortcut **CTRL+Y**.

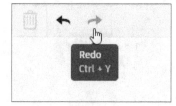

Figure-24. Redo tool

Group

The **Group** tool is used to combine shapes into a single object. The procedure to use this tool is discussed next.

- By default, the **Group** tool is inactive. To activate this tool, select two shapes in the workplane by holding the **Shift** key. The **Group** tool will be activated.
- Click on the **Group** tool from the toolbar or activate the tool by pressing the **Ctrl+G** key from keyboard; refer to Figure-25. The shapes will be combined into a single object; refer to Figure-26. If you now click on an object of the group then whole group will get selected. Also, the same properties like layer, color, etc. will be applied to all members of the group.

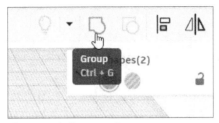

Figure-25. Group tool

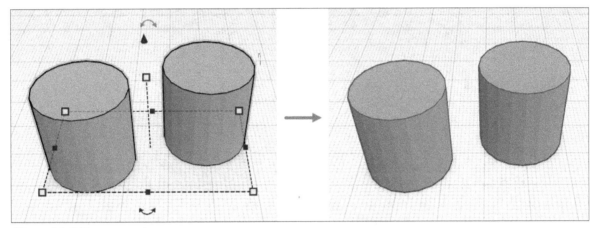

Figure-26. Objects grouped

Similarly, you can use the **Ungroup** tool to break selected group into individual objects.

Align

The **Align** tool is used to align the shapes. The procedure to use this tool is discussed next.

- By default, the **Align** tool is inactive.
- Select desired shapes in the workplane to be aligned by holding the **Shift** key. The **Align** tool will be activated.
- Click on the **Align** tool from the toolbar; refer to Figure-27. The Alignment handles will be displayed in the workplane; refer to Figure-28.

Figure-27. Align tool

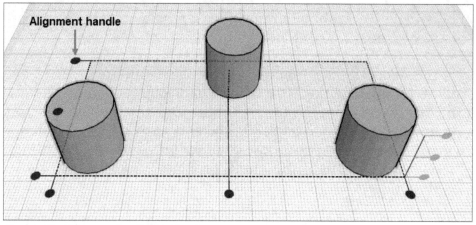

Figure-28. Alignment handles displayed

- Hover on desired alignment handle in the workplane on which the shapes are to be aligned, the preview of alignment of shapes will be displayed.
- Click on that alignment handle to align the shapes; refer to Figure-29.

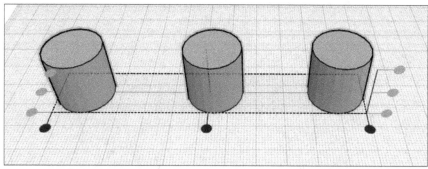

Figure-29. Shapes aligned

Mirror

The **Mirror** tool is used to create mirror image of selected object in defined direction. In simple words, this tool flips selected object in selected direction. The procedure to use this tool is discussed next.

- By default, the **Mirror** tool is inactive. To activate this tool, select desired shape from the workplane to be mirrored. The **Mirror** tool will be activated.
- Click on the **Mirror** tool from the toolbar; refer to Figure-30. The arrows will be displayed to define the direction in which mirror flip of object will be performed.

Figure-30. Mirror tool

- Hover the cursor on desired arrow. The preview of the mirrored shape will be displayed.
- Click on that arrow, the mirrored shape will be created; refer to Figure-31.

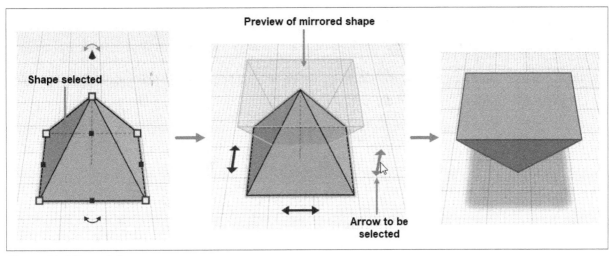

Figure-31. Mirrored shape

Cruise

The **Cruise** tool is used to place the shapes using specified reference point. Note that when you use the Cruise tool to move objects, the orientation of selected shapes also changes according to location where you are placing the objects. For example, if you are moving object on vertical wall then all the objects will be re-oriented perpendicular to vertical wall. The procedure to use this tool is discussed next.

- By default, the **Cruise** tool is inactive. To activate this tool, select desired shape which you want to relocate. The **Cruise** tool will be activated.
- Click on the **Cruise** tool from toolbar; refer to Figure-32. A dragging point will be displayed on the selected shape.

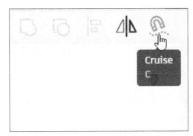

Figure-32. Cruise tool

- Click & drag the point at desired location and place it. The shape will be relocated; refer to Figure-33.

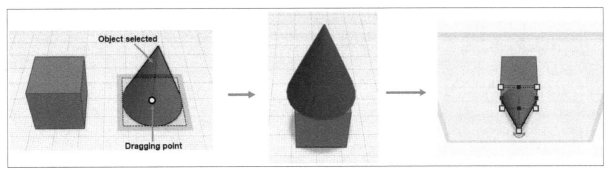

Figure-33. Shape placed

Import

The **Import** tool is used to import 2D and 3D files in the software. The procedure to use this tool is discussed next.

- Click on the **Import** tool from toolbar; refer to Figure-34. The **Import Shapes** dialog box will be displayed; refer to Figure-35.

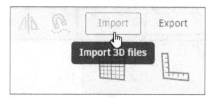

Figure-34. Import tool

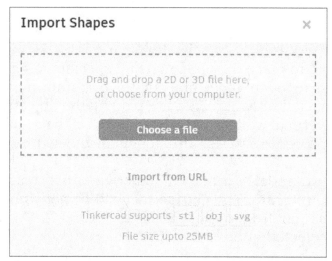

Figure-35. Import Shapes dialog box

- Click on the **Choose a file** button from the dialog box. The **Open** dialog box will be displayed; refer to Figure-36.

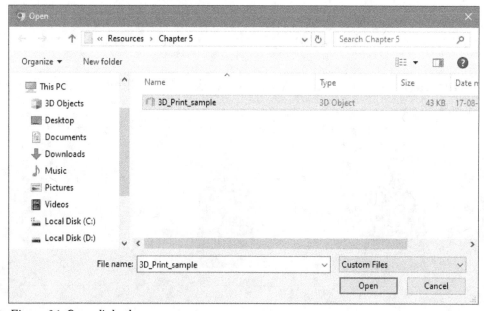

Figure-36. Open dialog box

- Select desired file from the dialog box and click on the **Open** button. The **Import 3D Shape** dialog box will be displayed with the attached imported file; refer to Figure-37. (Note that only **stl**, **obj**, and **svg** formats of file can be imported with upto only 25 MB of file size).

Figure-37. Import 3D Shape dialog box

- Select desired unit of measurement from **Units** area of the dialog box.
- Specify desired value in the **Scale** edit box to scale the shape.
- Specify desired values in the **Length**, **Width**, and **Height** edit boxes from **Dimensions** area.
- After specifying desired parameters, click on the **Import** button. The file will be imported as shape object; refer to Figure-38.

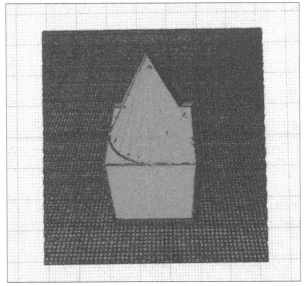

Figure-38. Import model

Export

The **Export** tool is used to export files in the selected formats. The procedure to use this tool is discussed next.

- Click on the **Export** tool from toolbar; refer to Figure-39. The **Export** dialog box will be displayed; refer to Figure-40.

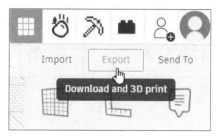

Figure-39. Export tool

Figure-40. Export dialog box

- Select **Everything in the design** radio button from **Include** area in the **Download** section to include all the files in the workplane to export. Select **The selected shape** radio button to include only the selected shapes to export.
- Click on the **Autodesk Fusion** button from **Take Your Designs Further with Autodesk** area and specify desired parameters to export the file to the software.
- On clicking desired formats of file in the **For 3D Print** and **For Lasercutting** area, the file will be downloaded on that format.
- Click on the **3D Print** section of the dialog box and specify desired parameters to print the file via desired 3D printer.

Send To

The **Send To** tool is used to share your design with people and apps. The procedure to use this tool is discussed next.

- Click on the **Send To** tool from the toolbar; refer to Figure-41. The **Send** dialog box will be displayed; refer to Figure-42.

Figure-41. Send To tool

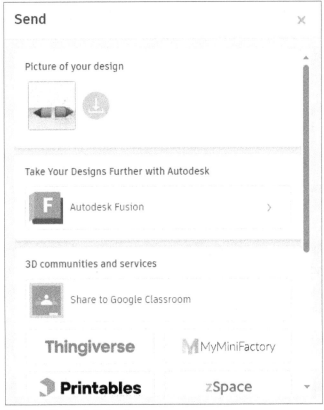

Figure-42. Send dialog box

- Click on the **Download locally** button from **Picture of your design** section to download the picture of the object currently on the workplane.
- Click on the **Autodesk Fusion** from **Take Your Designs Further with Autodesk** section to export the designs to the Autodesk Fusion.
- Select desired option from **3D communities and services** section to share the designs to the selected community.
- Click on the **Invite people** button from **Share over IM or email** section to share a link of your design to other people so that they can view and make changes to your design.

View Control

The **View Control** helps you to navigate and manipulate the view of the workspace. The tools are discussed next.

Home view

The **Home view** tool is used to reset the view to the default perspective view.

Fit all in view

The **Fit all in view** tool is used to centers and zooms the design so that it fits perfectly within the current workplane.

Zoom in

The **Zoom in** tool is used to magnify the view so that it becomes easier to work on fine details of the model.

Zoom out

The **Zoom out** tool is used to reduce the magnification so that you can see the larger portion of the workspace.

Switch to flat view (Orthographic)

The **Orthographic view** tool is used to display objects in their true size and shape, without any perspective distortion.

Switch to Perspective view

The **Perspective view** tool is used to display objects with a sense of depth, making objects easier to visualize how they will look in the real world.

Workspace Tabs

In the **3D Design** environment, the workspace tabs provide easy access to various tools and features that help to manage the designs and navigate the workspace effectively. These tabs are discussed next.

3D design

The **3D design** workspace tab is used to create and manipulate 3D models. This tab allow you to design anything from simple geometric shapes to complex structures.

Sim Lab

The **Sim Lab** workspace tab is used to apply gravity, forces, and materials to the 3D design and run the simulation.

Blocks

The **Blocks** workspace tab is used to display 3D design in the form of blocks. These blocks can be used in games like Minecraft.

Bricks

The **Bricks** workspace tab display the 3D design in the form of bricks. This workspace is useful for making lego blocks and puzzle games.

View Cube

The **View Cube** tool is a navigation tool that helps to control and change the viewpoint in the 3D workspace. It is particularly useful in orienting the model so that you can view and work on the model from any angle. To use View Cube, click & hold the **LMB** on the View Cube and drag the mouse. The object will rotate accordingly.

Settings

The **Settings** tool is used to specify desired parameters for the software. The procedure to use this tool is discussed next.

*   Click on the **Settings** tool from the work plane; refer to Figure-43. The **Workspace settings** dialog box will be displayed; refer to Figure-44.

Figure–43. Settings tool

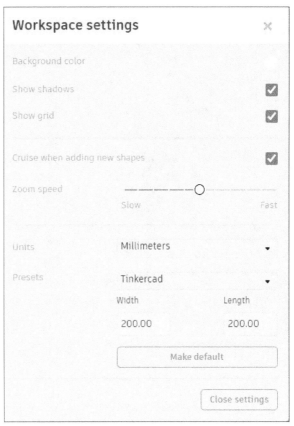

Figure–44. Workspace settings dialog box

*   Click on the **Background color** button, the **Solid colors** dialog box will be displayed to specify desired color of shape.
*   Select **Show shadows** check box to display the shadows of the shape.
*   Select **Show grid** check box to display the grid in the workplane.
*   Select **Cruise when adding new shapes** check box to cruise when placing the new shape.
*   Specify the zoom speed between slow and fast by dragging the **Zoom speed** dragger.
*   Specify desired unit from **Units** drop-down.
*   Specify desired preset for the workplane from **Presets** drop-down.
*   Enter desired value of width and length of the workplane in the **Width** and **Length** edit boxes.
*   Click on the **Make default** button to specify default values of all the parameters.

• After specifying desired parameters, click on the **Close settings** button to close the dialog box.

Workplane tool

The **Workplane** tool is an important feature that allows you to redefine the base surface on which you build or place objects. With the Workplane tool, it is easier to add or align new shapes, components, or text at different angles or elevations. The procedure to use this tool is discussed next.

• Click on the **Workplane** tool or press **W** key from keyboard and drag & click on any surface of the model where you want to place the new workplane. The new workplane will be placed and the workplane will becomes parallel to that surface; refer to Figure-45.

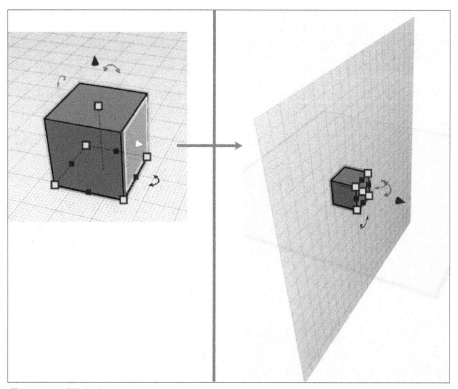

Figure–45. Workplane created

Ruler tool

The **Ruler** tool is an important feature for exact measurement and positioning within your 3D design workspace. The procedure to use this tool is discussed next.

• Click on the **Ruler** tool or press **R** key from keyboard and drag & place it on the workplane. The ruler will be placed; refer to Figure-46.
• Click on the circle button at the origin of scale as shown in Figure-46 to rotate the scale for changing orientation on plane.

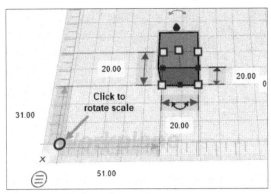

Figure-46. Ruler tool created

- Click on 🖹 button to toggle between midpoint or endpoint of the ruler.

BASIC SHAPES TOOLS

Select the **Basic Shapes** option from the **Shapes Library** drop-down. The tools related to basic shapes will be displayed; refer to Figure-47.

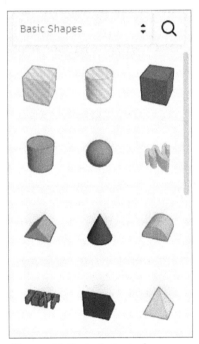

Figure-47. Basic shapes tools

Box

The **Box** tool is used to create box shape of specified size. The procedure to use this tool is discussed next.

- Click on the **Box** tool from **Basic Shapes** library and drag it to the workplane. The box shape will be placed and the **Box** dialog box will be displayed; refer to Figure-48. If you have selected the **Cruise when adding new shapes** check box from the **Workspace Settings** dialog box as discussed earlier then press **C** key to place objects on work plane and if you have not selected the check box from the **Workspace Settings** dialog box then press **C** key to place the objects on other objects (Cruise).

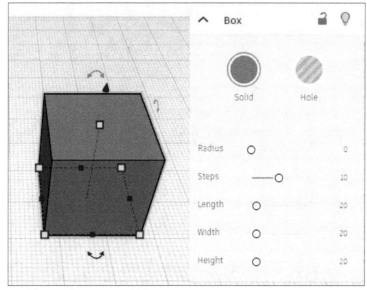

Figure-48. Box placed with Box dialog box

- Toggle the 🔓 button to lock or unlock the editing parameters in the dialog box.
- Click on the **Hide Selected** button from the dialog box to hide the selected shape and click on the **Show All** button from the toolbar to display the hidden shape.
- Click on the **Solid** button, the **Solid colors** dialog box will be displayed; refer to Figure-49.

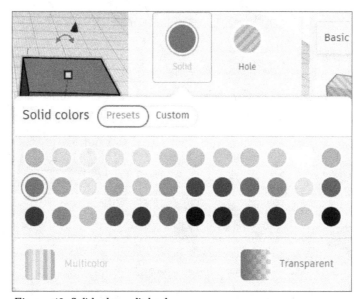

Figure-49. Solid colours dialog box

- Select desired color from **Presets** tab of the dialog box to be applied to the shape.
- Click on the **Custom** tab from the dialog box, the options will be displayed as shown in Figure-50.

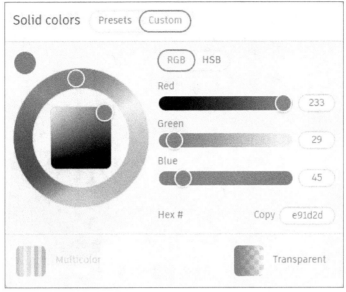

Figure-50. Custom tab

- Specify desired parameters in the dialog box to customize the color of shape.
- Click on **Transparent** button to make the shape transparent; refer to Figure-51.

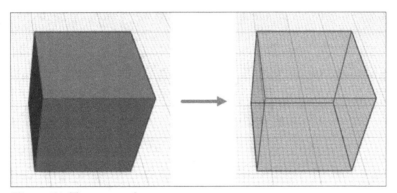

Figure-51. Transparent box

- Click on the **Hole** button from the dialog box, the shape will become hollow; refer to Figure-52.

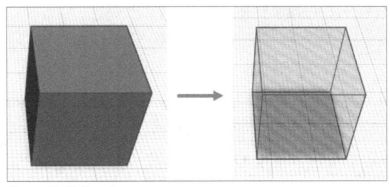

Figure-52. Hollow shape

- Specify desired values of length, width, and height of box in the **Length**, **Width**, and **Height** edit boxes, respectively or by using the respective slider.
- Specify desired value of fillet radius in the **Radius** edit box. This will make sharp edges of model round by specified radius.

- Specify desired value in the **Steps** edit box to define the number of faces to be created in the round edges when radius value is specified. If you set this value to 1 then chamfers will be applied on sharp edges of the model with length equal to specified radius; refer to Figure-53.

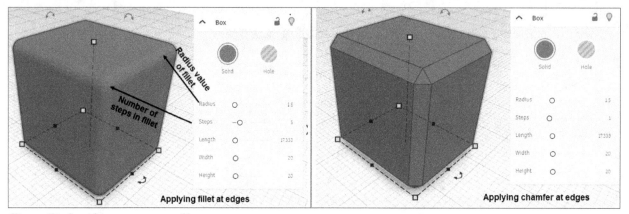

Figure-53. Specifying parameters of box

- After specifying desired parameters, click in the workplane to exit the dialog box.

Cylinder

The **Cylinder** tool is used to create cylinder shape. The procedure to use this tool is discussed next.

- Click on the **Cylinder** tool from **Basic Shapes** library and drag it to the workplane. The cylinder will be placed and the **Cylinder** dialog box will be displayed; refer to Figure-54.

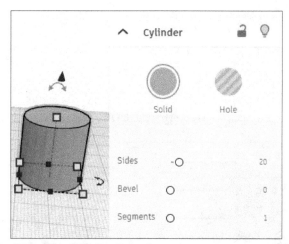

Figure-54. Cylinder dialog box

- Specify desired value in the **Sides** edit box to define the number of facets in the cylinder. More the number of sides, more the cylinder will be smoother.
- Specify desired value in the **Bevel** edit box to define the sloped edge or rounded corner to a shape.
- Specify desired value of **Segments** edit box to define the circular edge of the cylinder. More the number of segments, more the edge of the cylinder will be smoother; refer to Figure-55.

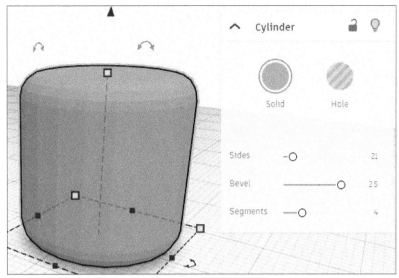

Figure-55. Specifying parameters of cylinder

- Specify other parameters in the dialog box as discussed earlier. Click in the workplane to exit the dialog box.

Scribble

The **Scribble** tool is used to create free-hand shapes. The procedure to use this tool is discussed next.

- Click on the **Scribble** tool from **Basic Shapes** library and drag it to the workplane. The workplane will become parallel to the screen with the editing parameters and preview window; refer to Figure-56.

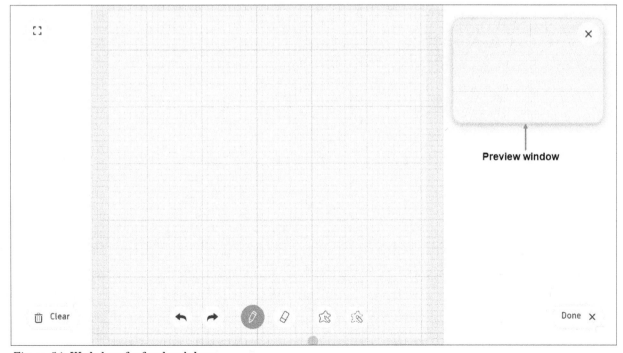

Figure-56. Workplane for free hand shape

- Create desired 2D shape in the workplane, the preview of 3D shape will be displayed in the preview window; refer to Figure-57.

Figure-57. Preview of 3D shape

- After creating desired shape, click on the **Done** button from scribble editing workplane. The 3D shape will be created and the **Scribble** dialog box will be displayed; refer to Figure-58.

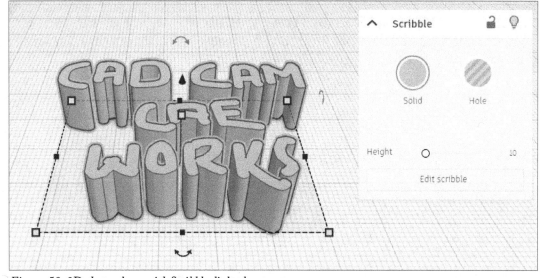

Figure-58. 3D shape along with Scribble dialog box

- Specify desired height of scribble in the **Height** edit box or by using the respective slider.
- Click on the **Edit scribble** button to enter into the editing environment.
- Specify other parameters in the dialog box as discussed earlier. Click in the workplane to exit the dialog box.

Cone

The **Cone** tool is used to place cone type structure in graphics area. The procedure to use this tool is discussed next.

- Click on the **Cone** tool from **Basic Shapes** library and drag it to the workplane. The cone will be placed and the **Cone** dialog box will be displayed; refer to Figure-59.

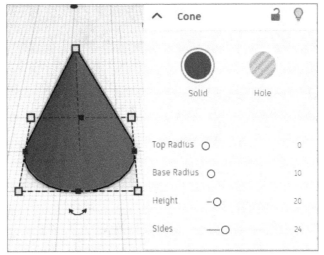

Figure-59. Cone dialog box

- Specify desired value in the **Top Radius** edit box to define the top radius of the cone which can be set to zero for a sharp point.
- Specify desired value in the **Base Radius** edit box to define the base radius of the cone.
- Specify desired value in the **Height** edit box to define the height of the cone.
- Specify desired value in the **Sides** edit box to define the number of facets in the cone; refer to Figure-60.

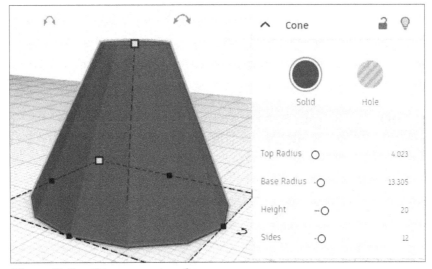

Figure-60. Specifying parameters of cone

- Specify other parameters in the dialog box as discussed earlier. Click in the workplane to exit the dialog box.

Text

The **Text** tool is used to create text of specified size and height. The procedure to use this tool is discussed next.

- Click on the **Text** tool from **Basic Shapes** library and drag it to the workplane. The text will be placed and the **Text** dialog box will be displayed; refer to Figure-61.

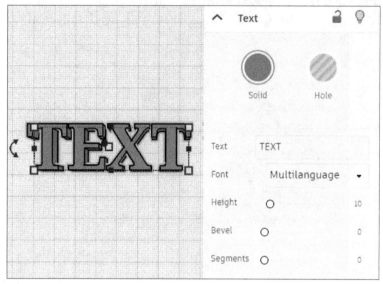

Figure-61. Text dialog box

- Specify desired text to be written in the **Text** edit box.
- Select desired font of text from **Font** drop-down.
- Specify desired height, bevel, and segments of text in the **Height**, **Bevel**, and **Segments** edit boxes, respectively or by using the respective slider.
- Specify other parameters in the dialog box as discussed earlier. Click in the workplane to exit the dialog box.

Similarly, you can use Half Sphere, Polygon, and Paraboloid tools.

Torus

The **Torus** tool is used to create torus shape. The procedure to use this tool is discussed next.

- Click on the **Torus** tool from **Basic Shapes** library and drag it to the workplane. The torus shape will be placed and the **Torus** dialog box will be displayed; refer to Figure-62.

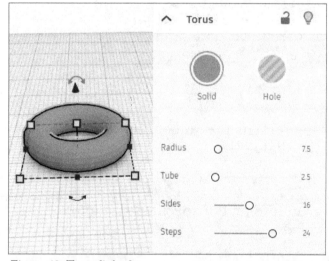

Figure-62. Torus dialog box

- Specify desired radius, tube, sides, and steps of torus in the **Radius**, **Tube**, **Sides**, and **Steps** edit boxes, respectively or by using the respective slider.

- Specify other parameters in the dialog box as discussed earlier. Click in the workplane to exit the dialog box.

Tube

The **Tube** tool is used to create tube like shape. The procedure to use this tool is discussed next.

- Click on the **Tube** tool from **Basic Shapes** library and drag it to the workplane. The tube shape will be placed and the **Tube** dialog box will be displayed; refer to Figure-63.

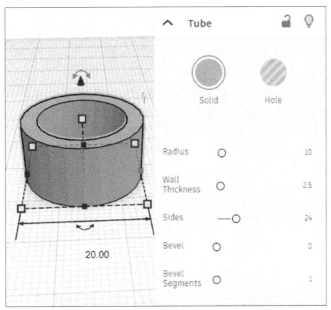

Figure-63. Tube dialog box

- Specify desired radius, wall thickness, sides, bevel, and bevel segments of tube in the **Radius**, **Wall Thickness**, **Sides**, **Bevel**, and **Bevel Segments** edit boxes, respectively, or by using the respective slider.
- Specify other parameters in the dialog box as discussed earlier. Click in the workplane to exit the dialog box.

Star

The **Star** tool is used to create star like shape. The procedure to use this tool is discussed next.

- Click on the **Star** tool from **Basic Shapes** library and drag it to the workplane. The star shape will be placed and the **Star** dialog box will be displayed; refer to Figure-64.

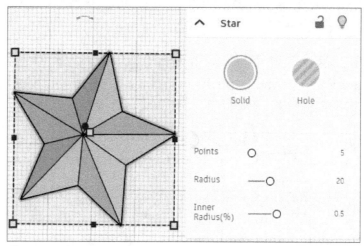

Figure-64. Star dialog box

- Specify desired value in the **Points** edit box to define the number of points on the star, ranging from a basic 5-point star to more complex designs.
- Specify desired value in the **Radius** edit box to define the overall size of the star.
- Specify desired value in the **Inner Radius** edit box to define the inner radius of the star to control the roundness of star's points; refer to Figure-65.

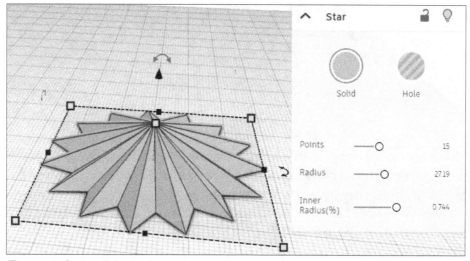

Figure-65. Star model created

Ring

The **Ring** tool is used to create ring like shape. The procedure to use this tool is discussed next.

- Click on the **Ring** tool from **Basic Shapes** library and drag it to the workplane. The ring shape will be placed and the **Ring** dialog box will be displayed; refer to Figure-66.

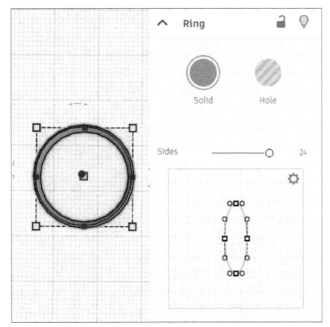

Figure-66. Ring dialog box

- Specify desired number of sides of ring in the **Sides** edit box or by using the respective slider.
- Modify the structure of ring by dragging the snapping points in the dialog box.
- Specify other parameters in the dialog box as discussed earlier. Click in the workplane to exit the dialog box.

Similarly, you can use **Sphere**, **Roof**, **Round Roof**, **Wedge**, **Pyramid**, **Half Sphere**, **Paraboloid**, **Heart**, **Star**, **Icosahedron**, **Dice**, and **Diamond** tools.

DESIGN STARTER TOOLS

Design Starters are pre-built 3D models to learn the basics of 3D modeling, helping users to overcome the fear of startiing from scratch. Select the **Design Starters** option from the **Shapes Library** drop-down to place objects like **Gifts**, **Storm Cloud**, and **Rounded Box**. The tools related to design starters will be displayed; refer to Figure-67.

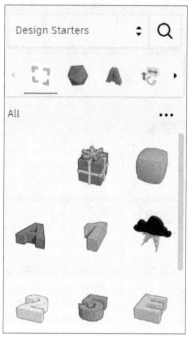

Figure-67. Design Starters tools

The procedure to use tools of **Design Starters** library is same as discussed for **Basic Shapes** library.

CREATURES AND CHARACTERS TOOLS

Creatures & Characters is a library of pre-built creature and character shapes, including humanoid figures, animals, toys, and other playful designs. Select the **Creatures & Characters** option from the **Shapes Library** drop-down to place objects like **Standy arms up**, **Blanky**, and **Elvis**. The tools related to creatures and characters will be displayed; refer to Figure-68.

Figure-68. Creatures & Characters tools

The procedure to use tools of **Creatures & Characters** library is same as discussed for **Basic Shapes** library.

VEHICLES AND MACHINES TOOLS

Vehicles & Machines is a library of components to create and modify with different types of mechanical devices, vehicles, or other machinery. Select the **Vehicles & Machines** option from the **Shapes Library** drop-down to place objects like **Tire**, **Rocket**, and **Wheel 63mm**. The tools related to vehicles & machines will be displayed; refer to Figure-69.

Figure-69. Vehicles and Machines library

The procedure to use tools of **Vehicles & Machines** library is same as discussed for **Basic Shapes** library.

STRUCTURES AND SCENERY TOOLS

Select the **Structures & Scenery** option from the **Shapes Library** drop-down to place object like **Evergreen Tree**, **Baby Tree**, and **Mountain with snow**. The tools related to structures & scenery will be displayed; refer to Figure-70.

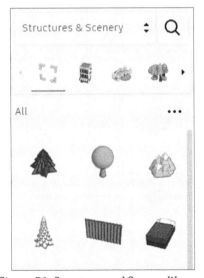

Figure-70. Structures and Scenery library

The procedure to use tools of **Structures & Scenery** library is same as discussed for **Basic Shapes** library.

HARDWARE TOOLS

Select the **Hardware** option from the **Shapes Library** drop-down to place object like **Snap-fit Gear**, **Chain**, and **Gear**. The tools related to hardware will be displayed; refer to Figure-71.

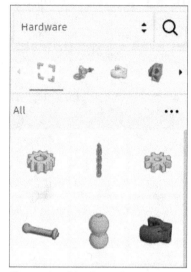

Figure-71. Hardware library

The procedure to use tools of **Hardware** library is same as discussed in **Basic Shapes** library.

ELECTRONICS TOOLS

Select the **Electronics** option from the **Shapes Library** drop-down to place object like **Peter Penguin for Glow Circuit Assembly**, **LED (10mm)**, and **Arduino Uno R3**. The tools related to electronics will be displayed; refer to Figure-72.

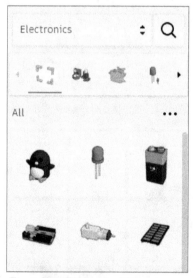

Figure-72. Electronics library

The procedure to use tools of **Electronics** library is same as discussed for **Basic Shapes** library.

FUN & GAMES TOOLS

Select the **Fun & Games** option from the **Shapes Library** drop-down to place object like **Skeleton Skull**, **Soccer Ball**, and **Christmas tree**. The tools related to fun & games will be displayed; refer to Figure-73.

Figure-73. Fun & Games library

The procedure to use tools of **Fun & Games** library is same as discussed for **Basic Shapes** library.

EVERYDAY OBJECTS TOOLS

Select the **Everyday Objects** option from the **Shapes Library** drop-down to place object like **Macbook Pro**, **Cell phone**, and **Water bottle**. The tools related to everyday objects will be displayed; refer to Figure-74.

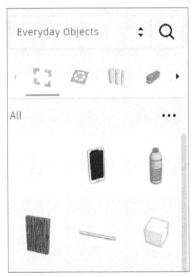

Figure-74. Everyday Objects library

The procedure to use tools of **Everyday Objects** library is same as discussed for **Basic Shapes** library.

FEATURED COLLECTIONS TOOLS

Select the **Featured Collections** option from the **Shapes Library** drop-down to place object like **Houseplant**, **Large seat**, and **Middle couch**. The tools related to featured collections will be displayed; refer to Figure-75.

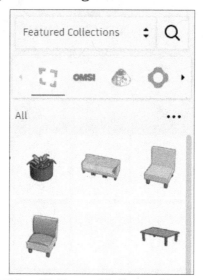

Figure-75. Featured Collections library

The procedure to use tools of **Featured Collections** library is same as discussed for **Basic Shapes** library.

SIM LAB TOOLS

Select the **Sim Lab** option from the **Shapes Library** drop-down to place object like **Pivot connector**, **Slider connector** and **Axle connector**. The tools related to simulation lab will be displayed; refer to Figure-76.

Figure-76. Sim Lab tools

The procedure to place shape of **Sim Lab** library is same as discussed for **Basic Shapes** library. Various tools in **Sim Lab** library to apply connectors are discussed next.

Pivot Connector

The **Pivot Connector** is a component used in 3D design of mechanical systems to create rotational joints in the model so that the 3D design can rotate about a fixed point in cone shaped boundary limits. The procedure to use this tool is discussed next.

- Click on the **Pivot Connector** tool from **Sim Lab** library and drag it to the workplane. The pivot connector will be placed and the **Pivot Connector** dialog box will be displayed; refer to Figure-77.

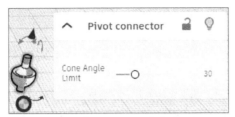

Figure-77. Pivot connector dialog box

- Specify desired cone angle limit of pivot connector in the **Cone Angle Limit** edit box or use respective slider to limit the range of motion; refer to Figure-78.

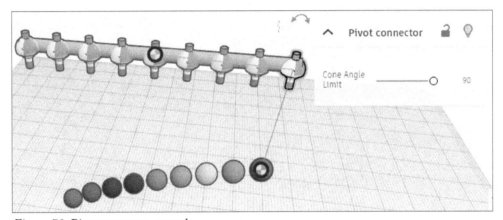

Figure-78. Pivot connectors example

- After specifying desired parameters, click in the work plane to exit the dialog box.

Slider Connector

The **Slider Connector** tool is used to create and simulate linear motion in your designs. This tool is useful for projects that involve parts moving along a straight path, such as sliders, pistons, or any mechanism requiring linear movement. The procedure to use this tool is discussed next.

- Click on the **Slider Connector** tool from **Sim Lab** library and drag it to the work plane. The slider connector will be placed and the **Slider Connector** dialog box will be displayed; refer to Figure-79.

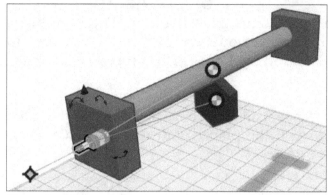

Figure-79. Slider connector example

- After specifying desired parameters, click in the work plane to exit the dialog box.

Axle Connector

The **Axle Connector** is a component used in 3D design of mechanical assemblies to create a connection between two parts so that one part will rotate around the axle while other part will support the axle. The procedure to use this tool is discussed next.

- Click on the **Axle Connector** tool from **Sim Lab** library and drag it to the workplane. The axle connector will be placed and the **Axle Connector** dialog box will be displayed; refer to Figure-80.

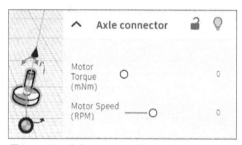

Figure-80. Axle connector dialog box

- Specify desired value in the **Motor Torque (mNm)** edit box or use the slider to define rotational force needed to rotate the object.
- Specify desired value in the **Motor Speed (RPM)** edit box to define the speed at which shaft/axle will rotate; refer to Figure-81.

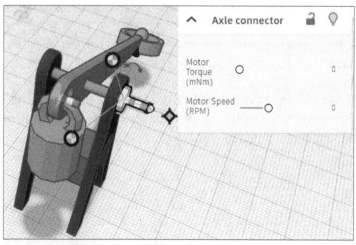

Figure-81. Axle connector example

- After specifying desired parameters, click in the workplane to exit the dialog box.

The procedure to use other tools in **Sim Lab** library is same as discussed in **Basic Shapes** library.

SHAPE GENERATORS TOOLS

Select the **Shape Generators** option from the **Shapes Library** drop-down. The tools related to shape generator will be displayed; refer to Figure-82. Select the **Featured** toggle button to access most commonly used shape generators. Select the **ALL** toggle button to access all the available shape generators.

Figure-82. Shape Generators library

SVG Revolver

The **SVG Revolver** tool is used to create revolve feature by using vector graphic saved in an svg file format. The procedure to use this tool is discussed next.

- Click on the **SVG Revolver** tool from **Shape Generators** library and drag it to the work plane. The component will be placed and the **SVG Revolver** dialog box will be displayed; refer to Figure-83.

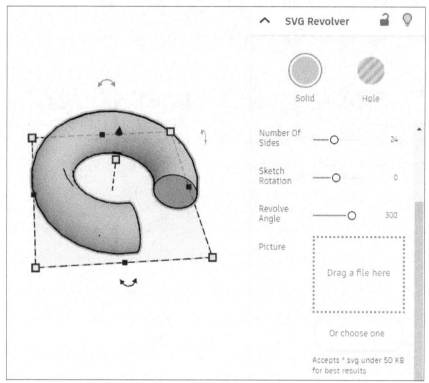

Figure-83. SVG Revolver dialog box

- Drag desired file of **.svg** format from the local drive for the **Picture** section of **SVG Revolver** dialog box or click on the **Or choose one** button. The **Open** dialog box will be displayed; refer to Figure-84.

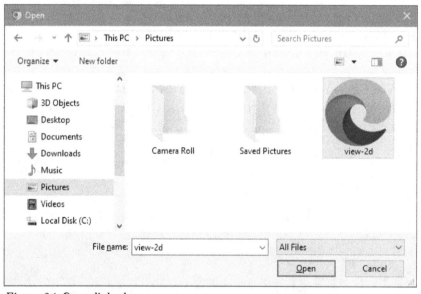

Figure-84. Open dialog box

- Select desired file of **.svg** format from the dialog box and click on the **Open** button. The file will be inserted and preview of revolve feature using vector graphic of selected file will be displayed; refer to Figure-85.

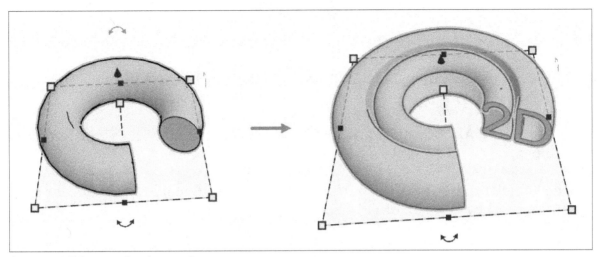

Figure-85. File inserted and executed

- The procedure to use other parameters in the dialog box is same as discussed in **Basic Shapes** library.
- After specifying desired parameters, click in the workplane to exit the dialog box.

Bent Pipe

The **Bent Pipe** tool is used to insert pipe with specified bend angle and shape in the workplane. The procedure to use this tool is discussed next.

- Click on the **Bent Pipe** tool from **Shape Generators** library and drag it to the workplane. The bent pipe will be placed and the **Bent Pipe** dialog box will be displayed; refer to Figure-86.

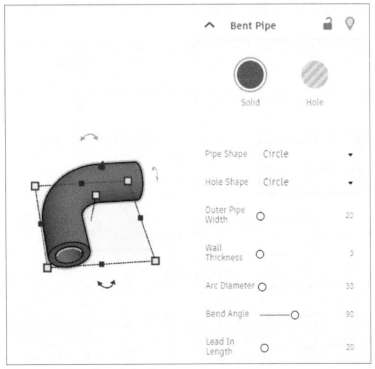

Figure-86. Bent Pipe dialog box

- Select desired shape of pipe and hole from **Pipe Shape** and **Hole Shape** drop-downs, respectively.

- The procedure to use other parameters in the dialog box is same as discussed in **Basic Shapes** library.
- After specifying desired parameters, click in the workplane to exit the dialog box.

The procedure to use other tools in **Shape Generators** library is same as discussed in **Basic Shapes** library.

All:- Click on the **All** button from the **Shape Generators** to access most commonly basic shapes.

Featured:- Click on the **Featured** button from the **Shape Generators** to access specific shapes designed by the Tinkercad users.

Search Shapes

The **Search shapes** tool is used to quickly find the specific shapes within the Shapes panel. The procedure to use this tool is discussed next.

- Click on the **Search shapes** $\boxed{Q}$ button from the **Tools Library**. The **Search shapes** box will be displayed; refer to Figure-87.
- Type the name of shape to be find in the **Search shapes** box. All the shapes related to the searched object will be displayed; refer to Figure-88.

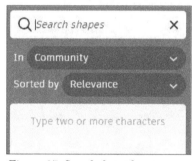

Figure-87. Search shapes box

Figure-88. Search results

- Select the **Community** option from **In** drop-down to find the shapes created by the Tinkercad community. Select the **Your Creations** option to find the shapes created by you.
- Select the **Relevance** option from **Sorted by** drop-down to sort the shapes in search results by matching closely with the searched object. Select the **Popular** option to sort the shapes in search results by the popularity of the shapes. Select the **Newest** option to sort the shapes in search results by the recently created shapes.

SIM LAB WORKSPACE

The **Sim Lab** workspace is used to apply gravity, forces, and materials to the 3D design and run the simulation. The procedure to use **Sim Lab** workspace is discussed next.

- Create a 3D design with the help of shapes in the **3D Design** workspace; refer to Figure-89.

Figure-89. 3D design created

- After creating desired 3D design, click on the **Sim Lab** tab from the toolbar. The **Sim Lab** workspace along with 3D design will be displayed; refer to Figure-90.

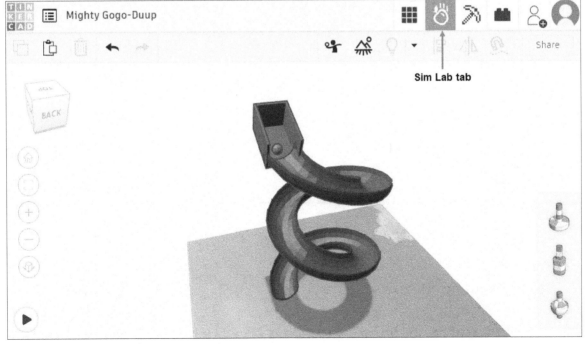

Figure-90. Sim Lab interface

- Click on the **Throwable objects**  button from the toolbar to throw virtual shapes to be simulated in the workplane and act as they are thrown physically. The **All Throwables** dialog box will be displayed; refer to Figure-91.

Figure-91. All Throwables dialog box

- While running the simulation, click in the workplane to throw random objects to interact with the design.
- Click on the **Scene settings** button from the toolbar to customize the appearance of 3D design workspace. The **Ground** dialog box will be displayed; refer to Figure-92.

Figure-92. Ground dialog box

- Click on the **Material** or **Color** button and select desired material or color for the ground in the workplane, respectively.
- Specify the gravity and shake amplitude of the ground by dragging the **Gravity** and **Shake Amplitude (mm)** slider from **Settings** rollout, respectively.

- On selecting any shape in the dialog box, the **Shape** dialog box will be displayed; refer to Figure-93.

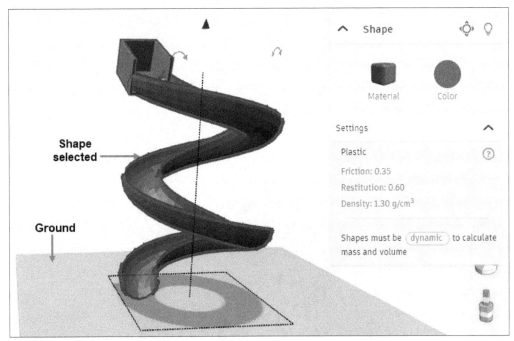

Figure-93. Shape dialog box on selecting the shape

- The **Settings** rollout displays the properties of the shape selected in the workplane. You can change the material and color of shape as discussed earlier from the panel.
- Toggle the ⬦ button to make the position of shape as dynamic or static. Select the **Dynamic** option to move the component during simulation and select the **Static** option to keep the component static during simulation.
- After specifying desired parameters, click on the **Play simulation** ▶ button from bottom left corner of the **Sim Lab** interface. The simulation of 3D design will be played; refer to Figure-94.

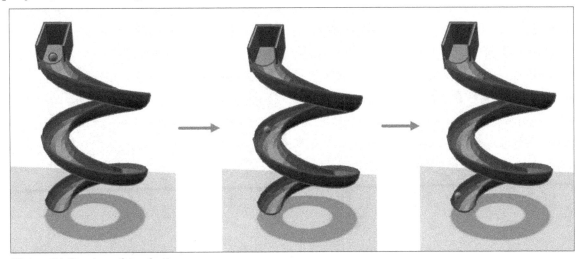

Figure-94. Preview of simulation

BLOCKS WORKSPACE

The **Blocks** workspace display the 3D design in the form of blocks. These blocks can be used in games like Minecraft. The procedure to use **Blocks** workspace is discussed next.

- First, create a desired 3D design with the help of shapes in the **3D Design** workspace as discussed earlier and click on the **Blocks** tab from the toolbar. The **Blocks** workspace will be displayed along with **Blocks** dialog box and 3D design in the form of blocks; refer to Figure-95.

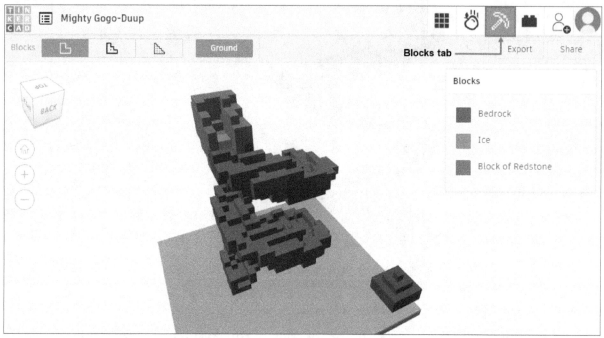

Figure-95. Blocks workspace

- Click on desired option in the **Blocks** dialog box and specify desired color for the blocks.
- Select [ ] , [ ] , or [ ] button from **Blocks** area in the **Blocks** workspace to define refinement of design in blocks; refer to Figure-96.

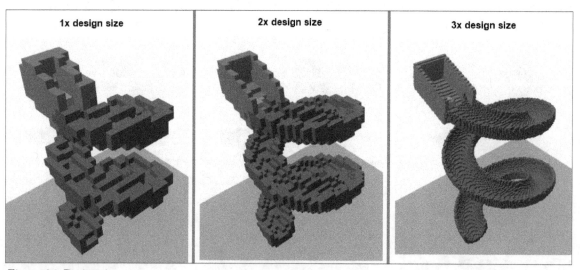

Figure-96. Design sizes

- Toggle the **Ground** button to display the ground in the workplane or not.

BRICKS WORKSPACE

The **Bricks** workspace display the 3D design in the form of bricks. This workspace is useful for making lego blocks and puzzle games. The procedure to use **Bricks** workspace is discussed next.

- First, create desired 3D design with the help of shapes in the **3D Design** workspace as discussed earlier and then click on the **Bricks** tab from the toolbar. The **Bricks** workspace will be displayed along with the 3D design in the form of bricks; refer to Figure-97.

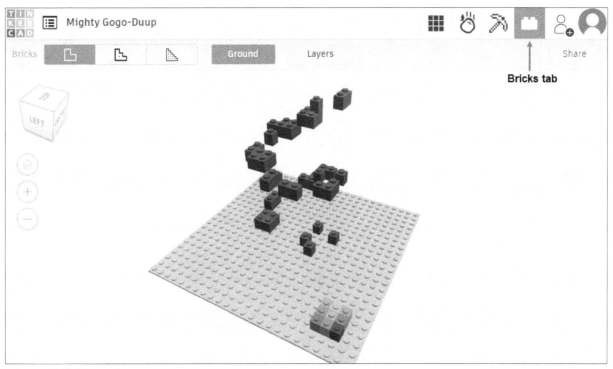

Figure-97. Bricks workspace

- Select desired button from **Bricks** area in the **Bricks** workspace to define refinement of design as discussed earlier; refer to Figure-98.

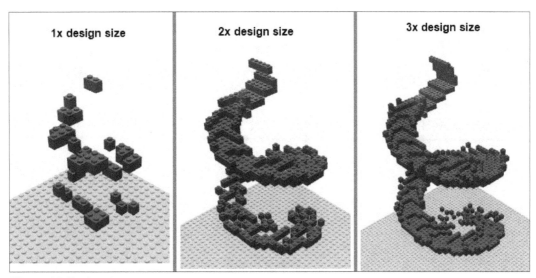

Figure-98. Design sizes

- Toggle the **Layers** button to display the 3D design in multiple layer of bricks so that you can create lego model of the design layer by layer in real world using lego blocks.

Invite people to design with you

- Click on the **Invite people to design with you** button from the **Workspace tabs**. The **Collaborate** dialog box will be displayed; refer to Figure-99.

Figure-99. Collaborate dialog box

- Click on the **Generate new link** button from the dialog box, the link will be generated and you will be asked to copy the link; refer to Figure-100.

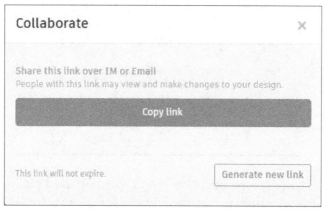

Figure-100. Link generated

- Click on the **Copy link** button, the link will be copied.
- Now, you can share the link via E-mail and other social media platforms.
- Once your team member click on that link, they will join the project and start tinkering. Note that only five users can collaborate on a single design at the same time.

PRACTICAL 1

Create the practical as shown in Figure-101.

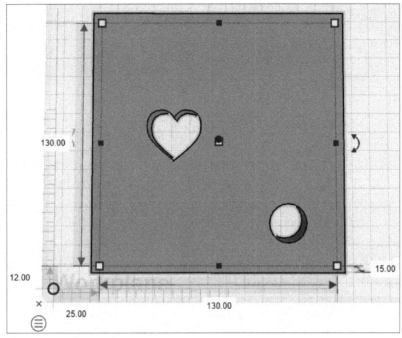

Figure-101. Practical 1

Steps

• Click on the **+Create** button from the application window, the three options will be displayed. Click on the **3D Design** button, the 3D Design workspace will be displayed.

• Place a ruler at the corner point as shown in Figure-101 by dragging the **Ruler** tool from **Panel** to workplane.

Note that you should always place ruler when starting a new design.

• Click on the **Box** tool from **Basic Shapes** library and drag it to the workplane. The box shape will be placed and the **Box** dialog box will be displayed; refer to Figure-102.

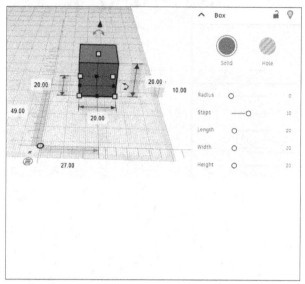

Figure-102. Box dialog box

- Specify the height, length, and width of the box as **15**, **130**, and **130**, in their respective edit boxes, or by using the respective sliders; refer to Figure-103.

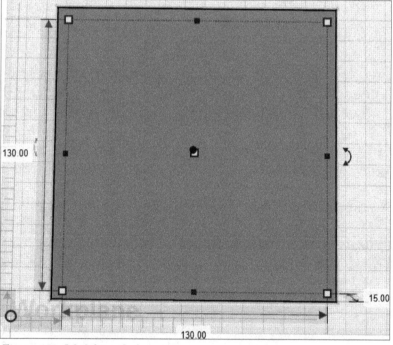

Figure-103. Modifying the box

- Click on the **Cylinder** tool and drag it on the box; refer to Figure-104.
- Select the cylinder shape and click on the handle in the model and drag it to the downwards up to the level where it cross the box shape as shown in Figure-104.

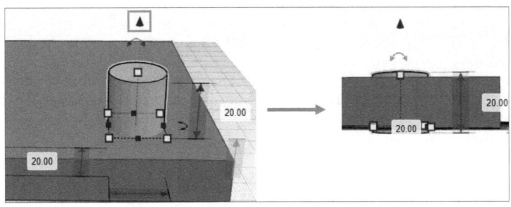

Figure-104. Cylinder dragging downwards in the box

- Select the cylinder shape and click on the **Hole** button from the **Cylinder** dialog box. The hole will be transparent; refer to Figure-105.

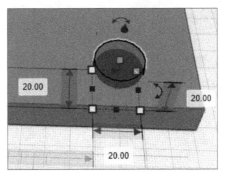

Figure-105. Cylinder shape hole created

- Now select both shapes from the workplane while holding the **SHIFT** key and click on the **Group** tool from the toolbar. The hole will be created.
- Similarly, create the hole of heart shape by using Heart tool in **Shapes** panel.

PRACTICAL 2

Create the practical as shown in Figure-106.

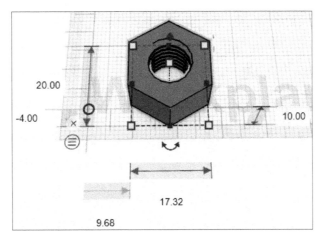

Figure-106. Practical 2

Steps

- Click on the **+Create** button from the application window, three options will be displayed. Click on the **3D Design** button, the 3D Design workspace will be displayed.
- Click on the **ISO Metric thread** tool from **Shape Generators** library and drag it to the workplane. The ISO metric thread will be placed and the **ISO metric thread** dialog box will be displayed; refer to Figure-107.

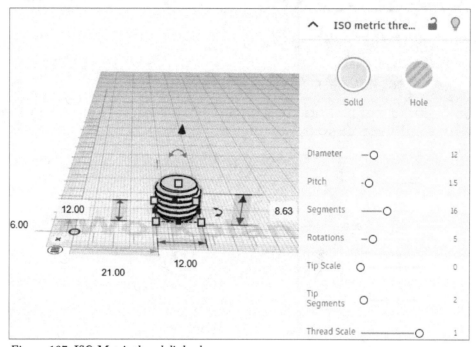

Figure-107. ISO Metric thread dialog box

- Specify rotation of ISO metric thread as **18** in the respective edit box, or by using the slider; refer to Figure-108.

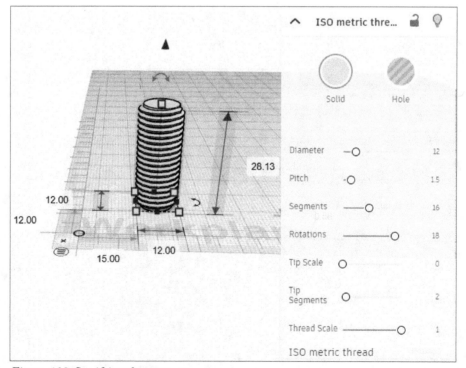

Figure-108. Specifying the parameters

- Click on the **Polygon** tool from **Basic Shapes** category in **Shapes** panel and drag it to the workplane in empty area. The polygon will be placed and the **Polygon** dialog box will be displayed.
- Specify height of the polygon as **10** in the model ; refer to Figure-109.

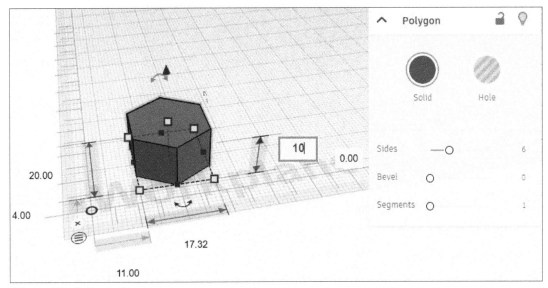

Figure-109. Polygon placed

- Select the **ISO Metric thread** shape and drag it on the polygon.
- Select the ISO Metric thread and click on the **Hole** button from the **ISO Metric thread** dialog box; refer to Figure-110.

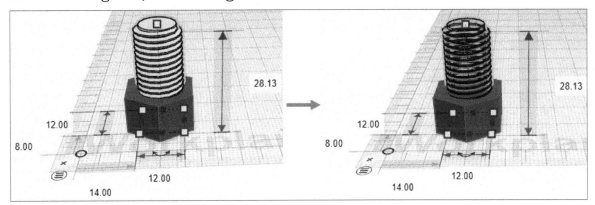

Figure-110. ISO metric thread drag on the polygon

- Now select both shapes from the workplane and click on the **Group** tool from the toolbar. The hole will be created.

PRACTICAL 3

Create the practical as shown in Figure-111.

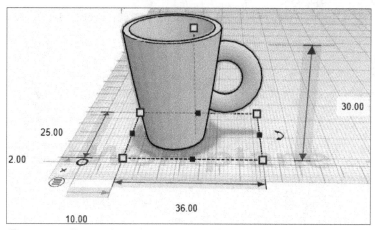

Figure-111. Practical 03

Steps

- Click on the **+Create** button from the application window, three options will be displayed. Click on the **3D Design** button, the 3D Design workspace will be displayed.
- Click on the **Paraboloid** tool and drag it to the workplane. The paraboloid shape will be placed and the **Paraboloid** dialog box will be displayed.
- Click on the **Box** tool and drag it on the paraboloid while holding the **C** key. Place the box in such a way that paraboloid is enveloped by it.
- Select the box and drag it to upwards by using the handle as shown in Figure-112 by **12mm** value.

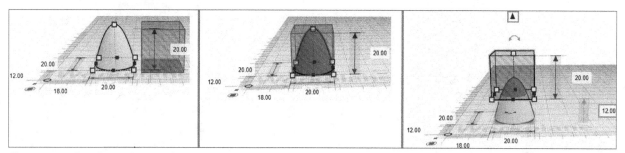

Figure-112. Box dragged upwards

- Select both shapes while holding the **SHIFT** key and click on the **Group** tool from the toolbar. The 3D design will be created as shown in Figure-113.

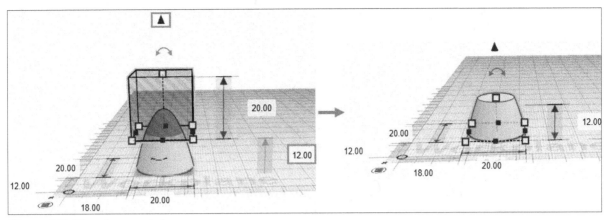

Figure-113. First shape created

- Select the shape and rotate it by **180⁰** by using rotation handle as shown in Figure-114.

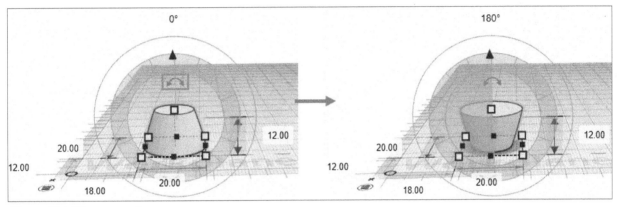

Figure-114. Shape rotated

- Specify height, length, and width of the paraboloid as **30**, **25**, and **25** in the workplane; refer to Figure-115.

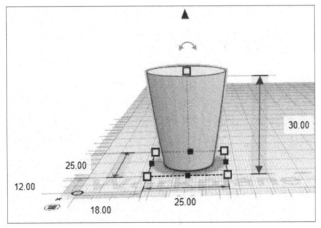

Figure-115. Specifying the parameters of shape

- Click on the **Torus** tool and drag it to the workplane. The torus shape will be placed and the **Torus** dialog box will be displayed.
- Specify height of the torus as **3** in the workplane.
- Select the shape and rotate it by **90°** by using rotation handle as shown in Figure-116.

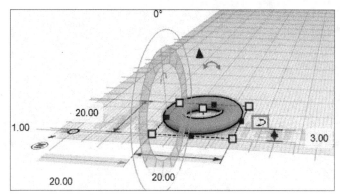

Figure-116. Rotating the torus

- Select the torus shape and drag it to upwards using handle displayed in the workplane so that the torus shape will lie on the workplane; refer to Figure-117.

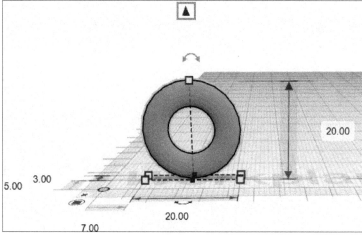

Figure-117. Torus shape dragged on the workplane

- Select the torus shape and set the parameters to move the torus as shown in Figure-118.

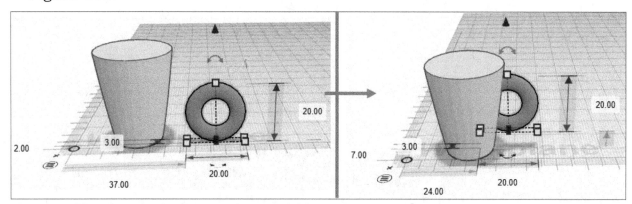

Figure-118. Torus shape placed at the center of paraboloid shape

- Select the both model while holding the **SHIFT** key then click on the **Group** tool from the toolbar. Both shapes will be grouped; refer to Figure-119.

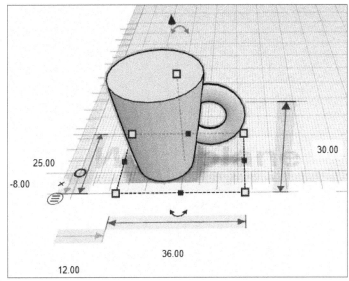

Figure-119. Group created

- Select the paraboloid shape and duplicate it by using the **Duplicate and Repeat** tool from the toolbar. Specify length, width, and height of the duplicated paraboloid as **22**, **23**, and **30**, respectively and drag the duplicate paraboloid inside of the paraboloid; refer to Figure-120.

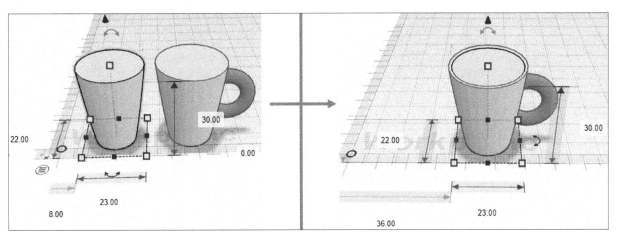

Figure-120. Specifying the parameters of duplicated paraboloid shape

- Select the duplicated paraboloid and drag it to upwards by using the handle displayed in the workplane by **3mm** as shown in Figure-121.

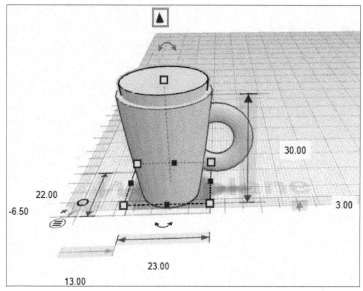

Figure-121. Dragging the duplicated paraboloid shape upwards

- Select both paraboloids and click on the **Align** tool from the toolbar. The editing points will be displayed. Click on the points as highlighted in Figure-116 to align both the paraboloids at the center; refer to Figure-122. Press **ESC** to exit the tool.

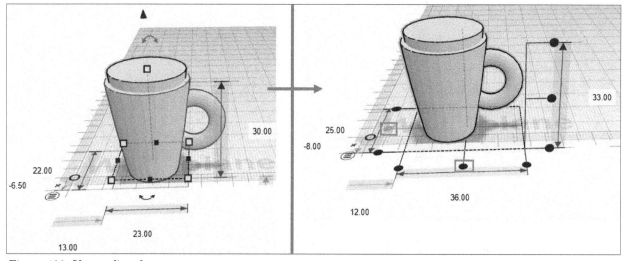

Figure-122. Shapes aligned

- Select the inner paraboloid shape and click on the **Hole** button from the **Paraboloid** dialog box. The inner paraboloid shape will be transparent.
- Now, select all the three shapes and click on the **Group** tool from the toolbar. The 3D design of cup will be created; refer to Figure-123.

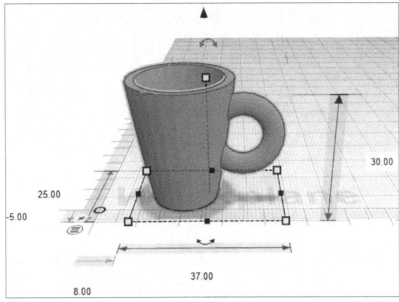

Figure-123. Practical 3 created

PRACTICAL 4

- Create the practical as shown in Figure-124.

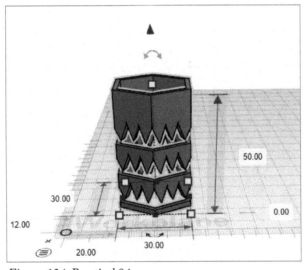

Figure-124. Practical 04

Step

- Start a new 3D design as discussed earlier.
- Click on the **Polygon** tool from the **Shapes** panel and drag it to the workplane. The polygon shape will placed and the **Polygon** dialog box will be displayed.
- Specify height, length, and width of the polygon as **50**, **30**, and **30** in the edit boxes displayed in the workplane.
- Select the polygon shape and click on the **Duplicate and Repeat** tool from the toolbar. The duplicate polygon will be created.
- Specify the length and width of duplicated polygon as **27** and the height remains same.

- Select both polygon shapes while holding the **SHIFT** key and click on the **Align** tool from the toolbar. The editing points will be displayed. Click on the points as discussed earlier to align both polygon shapes at the center.
- Select the inner polygon and click on the **Hole** button from the **Polygon** dialog box. The inner polygon will be transparent.
- Now, select both polygon shapes while holding **SHIFT** key and click on the **Group** tool from the toolbar. The shape will become hollow from inside; refer to Figure-125.

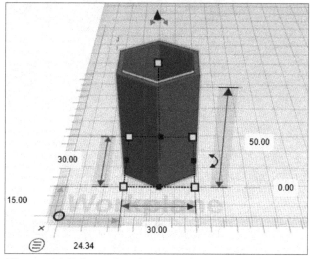

Figure-125. Polygon shape hole created

- Click on the **Roof** tool and drag it to the workplane. The roof will be placed and the **Roof** dialog box will be displayed.
- Specify length and width of the roof shape as **80** and **8** in the edit boxes displayed in the workplane; refer to Figure-126.

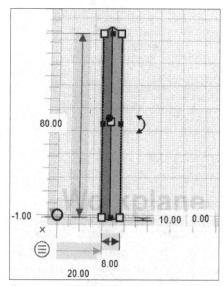

Figure-126. Roof shape created

- Select the roof shape and click on the **Duplicate and Repeat** tool from the toolbar. The roof shape will be duplicated.
- Select the duplicated shape and rotate it by **22.5°** by using rotate button displayed in the workplane and keep clicking on the **Duplicate and Repeat** tool until you get the patterned shape of roof as shown in Figure-127.

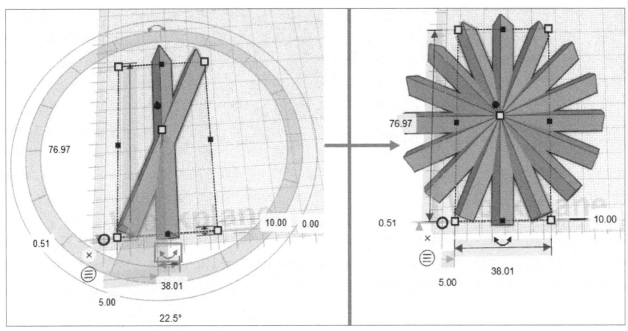

Figure-127. Patterned shape of roof created

- Now, select the newly created patterned roof shape and click on the **Group** tool from the toolbar. The shape will be grouped.
- Click & drag the polygon shape on the patterned roof shape; refer to Figure-128. You can switch to **Top** view by using **ViewCube** for better view.

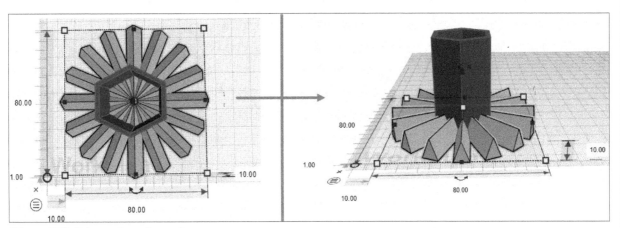

Figure-128. Polygon shape dragged

- Select the patterned roof shape and drag it to upwards by **2mm** using the handle to displayed in the workplane; refer to Figure-129.

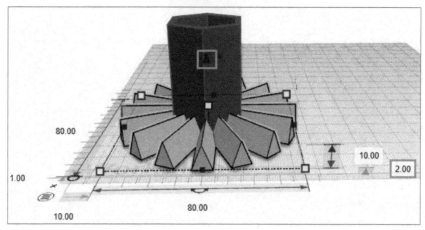

Figure-129. Dragging the Roof shape upwards

- Select the patterned roof shape and click on the **Duplicate and Repeat** tool twice from the toolbar. The patterned roof shape will be duplicated twice.
- Select the duplicated patterned roof shapes one by one and move them upward with **15** mm gap between two consecutive pattern shapes. The shape will be created as shown in Figure-130.

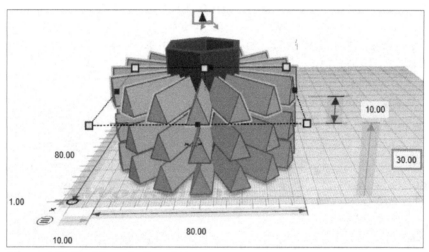

Figure-130. Roof shape duplicated

- Select all the patterned roof shapes by holding the **SHIFT** key and click on the **Hole** button from the **Roof** dialog box; refer to Figure-125. The shapes will become transparent; refer to Figure-131.

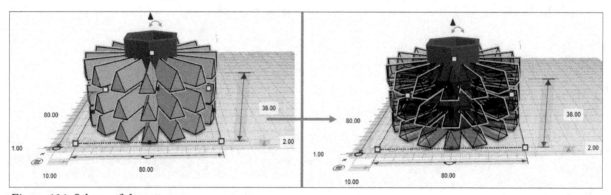

Figure-131. Select roof shape pattern

- Now, select all the shapes in the workplane and click on the **Group** tool from the toolbar. The 3D design of stand will be created; refer to Figure-132.

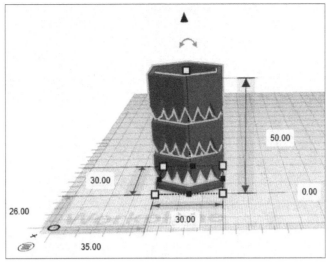

Figure-132. 3D model created

PRACTICAL 5

Create a **Spanner** in the workplane; refer to Figure-133.

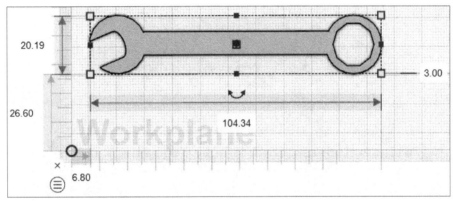

Figure-133. Practical 5

Steps

- Start a new 3D design as discussed earlier.
- Click on the **Cylinder** tool and drag it to the workplane. The cylinder shape will be placed and the **Cylinder** dialog box will de displayed.
- Specify height of the cylinder as **3** mm in the edit box displayed in the workplane.
- Click on the **Box** tool and drag it inside the cylinder in the workplane as shown in Figure-134.
- Select the box and click on the **Hole** button from the **Box** dialog box and specify width and length of the box as **12** mm and **15** mm; refer to Figure-134.

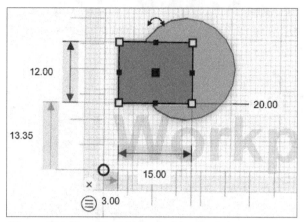

Figure-134. Dragging the box inside cylinder

- Select both shapes while holding the **SHIFT** key and click on the **Group** tool from the toolbar. The hole will be created; refer to Figure-135.

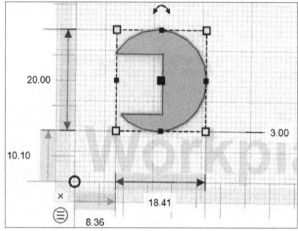

Figure-135. Hole created

- Click on the **Cylinder** tool and drag it inside the shape recently created; refer to Figure-136. Specify width and length of the cylinder as **7.30** mm and **12** mm in the edit boxes displayed in the workplane.
- Select the cylinder and click on the **Hole** button from the **Cylinder** dialog box; refer to Figure-136.

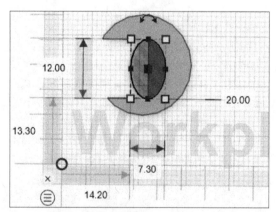

Figure-136. Cylinder drag inside model

- Select both shapes while holding the **SHIFT** key and click on the **Group** tool from the toolbar. A new shape will be created; refer to Figure-137.

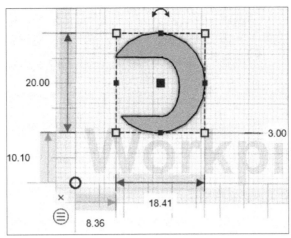

Figure-137. Cylinder shape created

- Select the cylinder and click on the rotate handle displayed in the workplane and rotate it as shown in Figure-138.

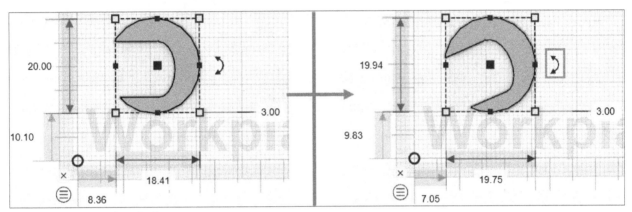

Figure-138. Rotate the cylinder

- Click on the **Box** tool and drag it to the workplane. The box shape will be placed and the **Box** dialog box will de displayed.
- Specify width, length, and height of the box as **8**, **68**, and **3**, respectively in the **Box** dialog box.
- Drag the box inside the shape recently created as shown in Figure-139.

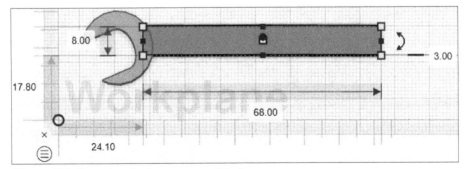

Figure-139. Dragging the box at center of circle

- Select both shapes while holding the **SHIFT** key and click on the **Group** tool from the toolbar. Both shapes will be grouped; refer to Figure-140.

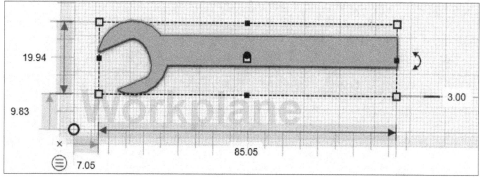

Figure-140. Group created

- Click on the **Tube** tool and drag it to the workplane. The tube shape will be placed and the **Tube** dialog box will de displayed.
- Specify height of the tube as **3** mm in the edit box displayed in the workplane.
- Specify the **Wall Thickness** of the tube as **4.05mm** in the **Tube** dialog box.
- Click on the **Polygon** tool and drag it inside the tube and specify the length and width of polygon as **16.17** mm and **14** mm, respectively in the edit box displayed in the workplane; refer to Figure-141.

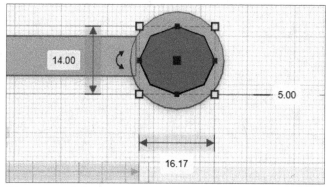

Figure-141. Polygon drag inside the tube

- Select the polygon and click on the **Hole** button from the **Polygon** dialog box and specify the **Sides** as **8** in the dialog box.
- Select tube and polygon shapes recently created while holding the **SHIFT** key and click on the **Group** tool from the toolbar. The hole will be created; refer to Figure-142.
- Drag the recently created shape at other end of the box as shown in Figure-142.

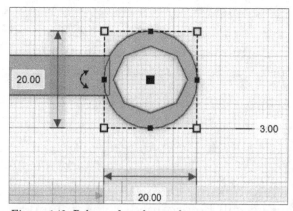

Figure-142. Polygon shaped created

- Select both shapes while holding the **SHIFT** key and click on the the **Group** tool from the toolbar. Both shapes will be grouped and the Spanner will be created; refer to Figure-143.

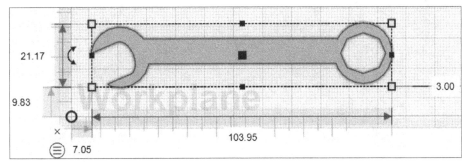

Figure-143. Spanner model created

PRACTICAL 6

Create the **kitchen** in the workplane; refer to Figure-144.

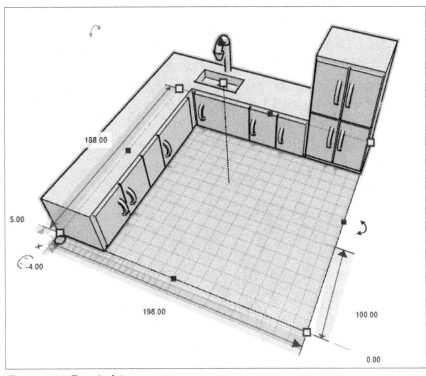

Figure-144. Practical 6

Steps

- Start a new 3D design as discussed earlier.
- Click on the **Box** tool and drag it to the workplane. The box shape will be placed and the **Box** dialog box will be displayed.
- Specify height, length, and width of the box shape as **100**, **50**, and **40**, respectively.
- Drag the box shape at the corner of the workplane.
- Select the box shape and click on the **Duplicate and Repeat** tool from the toolbar. The box shape will be duplicated.
- Specify the height, length, and width of the duplicated box shape as **45**, **40**, and **23**, respectively.
- Join the shapes as shown in Figure-145.

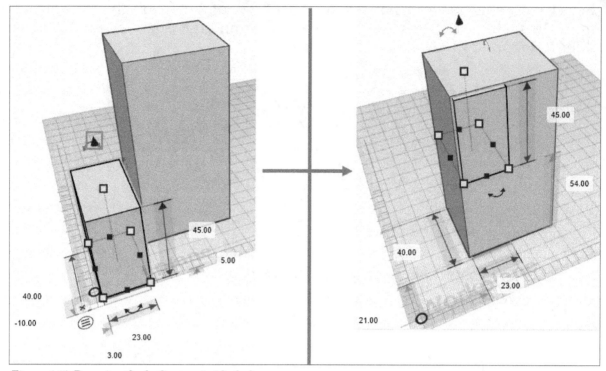

Figure-145. Dragging the duplicate to inside the box

- Select the duplicated box shape and click on the **Duplicate and Repeat** tool from the toolbar. The box shape will be duplicated.
- Select the newly created duplicated box shape and move the box using handle to displayed in the workplane as shown in Figure-146.

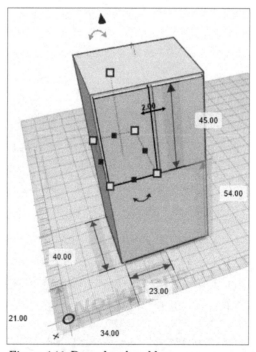

Figure-146. Drag the selected box

- Select both the duplicated box shapes and click on the **Duplicate and Repeat** tool from the toolbar. The box shapes will be duplicated.
- Now, select the new duplicated box shapes and drag it to downwards using the handle displayed in the workplane as shown in Figure-147.

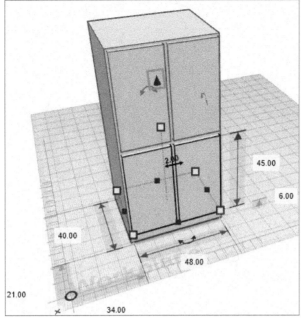

Figure-147. Dragging the box downside

- Click on the **Tube** tool and drag it to the workplane. The tube shape will be placed.
- Select the tube shape and specify the height and width of the shape as **2** mm and **10** mm, respectively in the edit box displayed in the workplane.
- Select the tube shape and rotate it about **90°** and drag it on the workplane using the handles displayed in the workplane.
- Now, drag the tube shape inside the box shape as shown in Figure-142 and click on the **Duplicate and Repeat** tool from the toolbar. The tube shape will be duplicated.
- Click & drag the duplicated tube shape as shown in Figure-148.

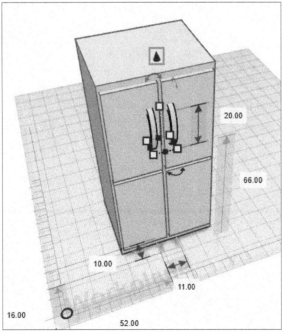

Figure-148. Drag the duplicate tube

- Select both the tube shapes using **SHIFT** key and click on the **Duplicate and Repeat** tool from the toolbar. The tube shapes will be duplicated.

- Select the newly duplicated tube shapes and drag it to downwards using the arrow key displayed in the workplane as shown in Figure-149.

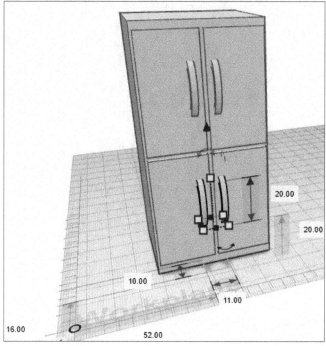

Figure-149. Drag the tube downside

- Click on the **Box** tool and drag it on the workplane adjacent to earlier created box. The box shape will be placed and the **Box** dialog box will be displayed.
- Drag and place the box to specify the length, width, and height as **148**, **40**, and **40**, respectively; refer to Figure-150.

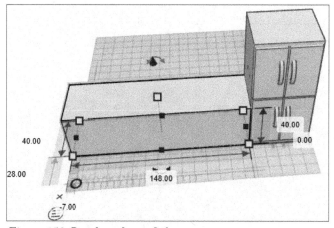

Figure-150. Box drag the workplane

- Select the newly created box shape and click on the **Duplicate and Repeat** tool. The newly created box shape will be duplicated.
- Make sure newly duplicated box is selected and drag it downwards using the down arrow key from the keyboard and rotate it about **90⁰** using the rotate handle displayed in the workplane. Now, drag the duplicated box shape as shown in Figure-151.

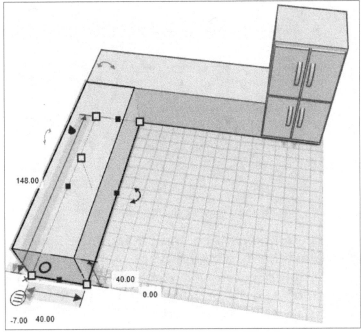

Figure-151. Drag and rotate the box

- Select both the recently created box shapes while holding the **SHIFT** key and click on the **Group** tool from the toolbar. The shapes will be grouped as shown in Figure-152.

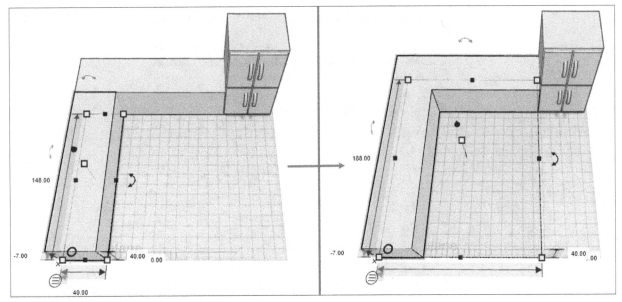

Figure-152. Selected box joints

- Click on the **Box** tool and drag it to the workplane. The box shape will be placed and the **Box** dialog box will be displayed.
- Specify the height, width, and length as **35**, **20**, and **26**, respectively.
- Select the recently created box shape and drag it inside the previously created box shape as shown in Figure-153.

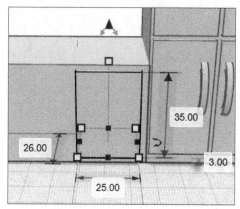

Figure-153. Dragging the duplicate box

- Select the recently created box shape and click on the **Duplicate and Repeat** tool twice. The box shape will be duplicated twice.
- Now, drag & place the duplicated box shapes side by side as discussed earlier and specify the length of second duplicated shape as **40** in the edit box displayed in the workplane as shown in Figure-154.

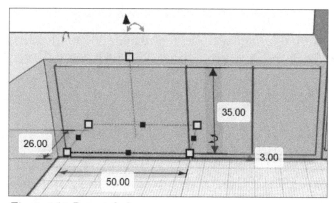

Figure-154. Repeat the boxes

- Similarly, create the box shapes inside the other earlier duplicated large box; refer to Figure-155.

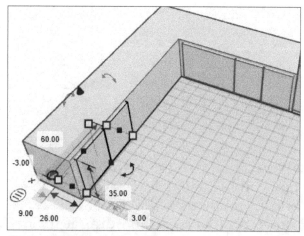

Figure-155. Drag inside the box

- Click on the **Transparent Box** tool and drag it at the location shown in Figure-156.

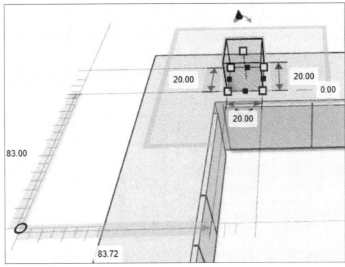

Figure-156. Transparent box place

- Specify length and width of the transparent box as **40** and **20**, respectively.
- Select the box and drag it to the distance of **-5** using the arrow button displayed in the workplane; refer to Figure-157.

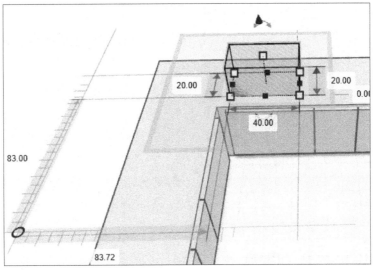

Figure-157. Transparent box drag box

- Select both the box shapes and click on the **Group** tool from the toolbar. The shape will be hollowed as shown in Figure-158.

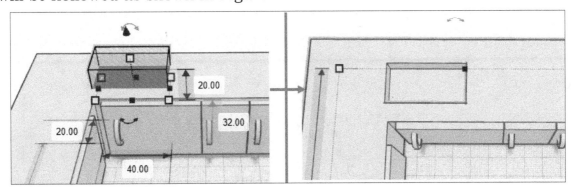

Figure-158. Hole created

- Click on the **Torus** tool and drag it on the hollowed area.

- Specify both the length and width as **15mm** in the edit boxes displayed in the workplane and select the **Hole** button in the **Torus** dialog box.
- Drag the torus shape downwards upto **-3mm** using handle as discussed earlier.
- Select both the box shape and torus shape joined while holding the **SHIFT** key and click on the **Group** tool. The hollow of torus shape will be created; refer to Figure-159.

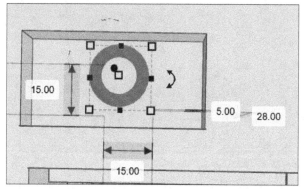

Figure-159. Torus created

- Click on the **Torus** tool and drag it to the workplane in an empty area.
- Click on the **Box (Hole)** tool and drag it over the torus shape as shown in Figure-154 while holding the **C** key.
- Select both shapes and click on the **Group** tool. The half shape of torus will be created; refer to Figure-160.

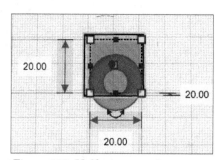

Figure-160. Half torus created

- Click on the **Cylinder** tool (Solid) and drag it to the workplane. Specify the height, width, and length as **30, 4,** and **4** respectively.
- Select the recently created half torus shape and rotate it about **90°** using rotate button as discussed earlier.
- Drag the half torus shape on the top of the cylinder as shown in Figure-161.

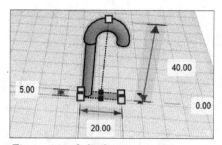

Figure-161. Cylinder torus model

- Select both shapes and click on the **Align** tool from the toolbar. The editing points will be displayed. Click on the points to align both the shapes at the center.
- Click on the **Cone** tool and drag it to the workplane.

- Specify the **Top Radius** of cone as **22** in the Cone dialog box and specify height, width, and length as **6, 5,** and **8,** respectively in the edit boxes displayed in the workplane.
- Select both torus and cone shapes and click on the **Align** tool from the toolbar. The editing points will be displayed. Click on the points to align both the shapes at the center; refer to Figure-162.

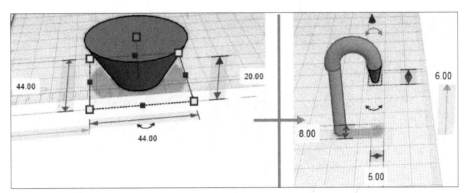

Figure-162. Cone join torus

- Select all the three shapes while holding **SHIFT** key and click on the **Group** tool from the toolbar. The shapes will be grouped.
- Now, drag the recently created shape as shown Figure-163. The 3D design of kitchen will be created.

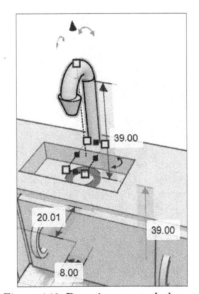

Figure-163. Dragging tap on the box

PRACTICES

Create practice models as shown in Figure-164, Figure-165, Figure-166, and Figure-167.

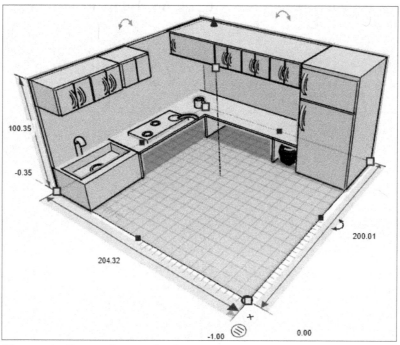

Figure-164. Practice drawing for 3D design

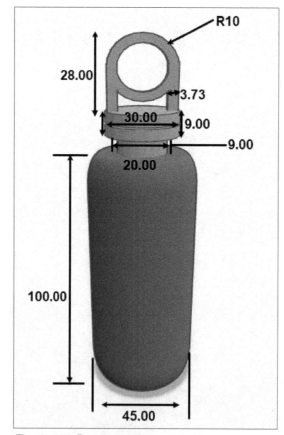

Figure-165. Practice 2

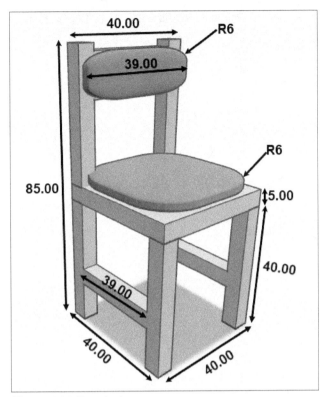

Figure-166. Practice 3

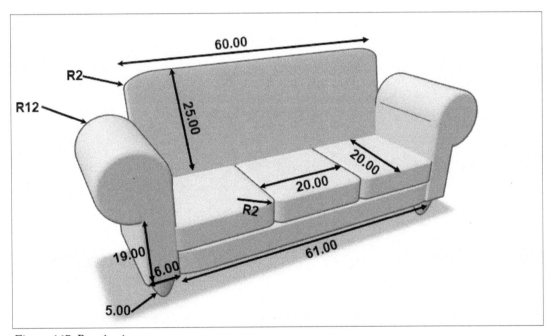

Figure-167. Practice 4

FOR STUDENTS NOTES

Chapter 2

Code Blocks

Topics Covered

The major topics covered in this chapter are:

- *Introduction to Code Blocks*
- *Starting with Code Blocks*
- *User Interface of Codeblocks*
- *Use Codeblocks Templates*
- *Working with Blocks in Shapes Library*
- *Working with Blocks in Control Library*
- *Working with Blocks in Math Library*
- *Working with Blocks in Variables Library*
- *Working with Blocks in Template Library*
- *Working with Blocks in Mark Up Library*
- *Working with Blocks in Legacy Library*
- *Practical and Practice*

INTRODUCTION

In previous chapter, we have discussed about the **3D Design** related tools. We have created various solid models and performed their simulations. In this chapter, we will discuss about **Code Blocks**. Code blocks are the pieces of programming codes that can be combined to create 3D models in Tinkercad. You can use these code blocks to place basic shapes, apply modifiers, use mathematical expressions to link dimensions of objects and perform other related tasks to leverage the power of programming in creating model. The procedure to start Code Blocks interface is given next.

STARTING CODE BLOCKS

* Click on the **+Create** button from the application window, the three options will be displayed; refer to Figure-1. Click on the **Codeblocks** button, the Codeblocks workspace will be displayed; refer to Figure-2.

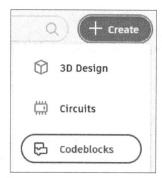

Figure-1. Create drop-down

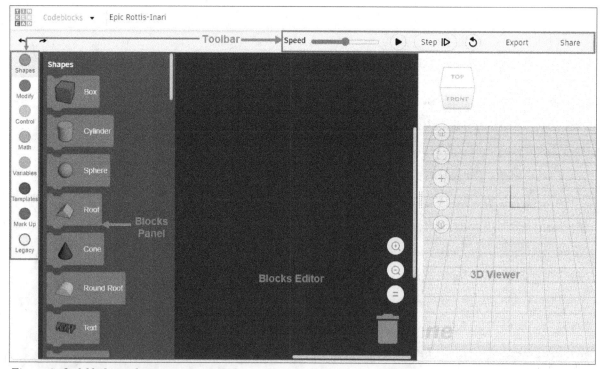

Figure-2. Codeblocks workspace

USER INTERFACE

The user interface of **Codeblocks** workspace contains Toolbar, Blocks panel, Block Editor, and 3D viewer; refer to Figure-2. The applications of these interface elements are discussed next.

Toolbar

The toolbar of **Codeblocks** workspace is divided into two segments. The toolbar at the left in application window contains tools to access categories of blocks in Blocks panel. For example, all the blocks related to modifying objects will be displayed on selecting **Modify** tool from the left toolbar. The horizontal toolbar below the Title bar of application window is used to access tools to perform operations like executing codes, exporting the model, sharing the model, and so on; refer to Figure-3. The functions of various tools are discussed next.

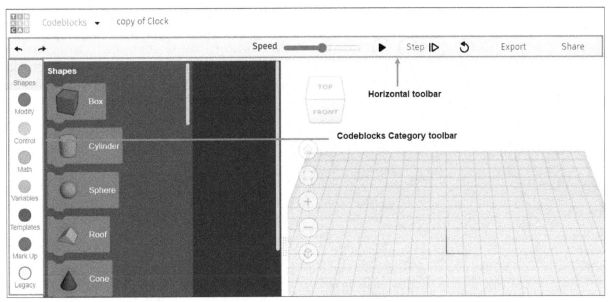

Figure-3. Toolbars in Codeblocks workspace

Speed Slider

• The **Speed** slider is used to define the speed at which codeblocks will be executed for creating model. Drag the slider towards left to slow the speed and to the right to increase the speed of execution.

Play Tool

• Click on the **Play** tool from the toolbar to run the execution of codeblocks.

Step Tool

• Click on the **Step** tool from the toolbar to run execution of codeblocks step by step. You can use this tool to find codeblocks which are causing error in execution or which are not functioning as intended as you have better control on execution of codes.

Reset Tool

• Click on the **Reset** tool ↻ from the toolbar to reset the 3D Viewer. This will clean the output model generated in 3D Viewer on execution of codeblocks.

Exporting File

The **Export** tool is used to export current model in specified CAD/Graphics format like STL, OBJ, SVG, and so on. The procedure to use this tool is given next.

*   Click on the **Export** tool from the toolbar. The **Export** dialog box will be displayed; refer to Figure-4.
*   Click on the **.STL** button to download the current model in STL file format. STL abbreviation of stereolithography is the format generally used by 3D printing software, Engineering analysis software, and other design software that can work on mesh objects. This is one of the most widely used format for 3D printing.
*   Click on the **.OBJ** button to download the current model in OBJ file format. OBJ format is open geometry definition file format first developed by Wavefront Technologies. Note that when you click on this button then a Zip file is generated which contains OBJ file of current model and a .MTL file which contains data related to color and material of the model. This format is mostly used by animation software.
*   Click on the **GLTF (.glb)** button from the dialog box if you want to export the model in minimum size format. Using this format also ensures fast unpacking on model data when importing in other software like **Sketchfab** and **Facebook**.

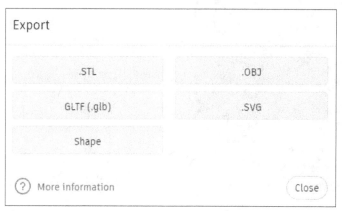

Figure-4. Export dialog box

*   Click on the **.SVG** button from the dialog box to download current model in Scalable Vector Graphics (SVG) format. This format is mostly used in laser cutting machines or tools that follow curves to perform actions. Note that vector graphics do not loose quality or pixelate when zooming in.

Exporting as Shape

*   Click on the **Shape** button from the dialog box to save current model as a shape in **Shapes** panel of **3D Design** workspace so that you can reuse the shape later. On doing so, the **Create Shape** window will be displayed; refer to Figure-5.
*   Specify desired name of the shape by which you want to find it in **Shapes** panel of **3D Design** workspace.
*   Specify desired text description about the shape in the **Description** edit box. The text can be used to provide tips or purpose of the shape.
*   Specify desired keywords for the shape in **Tags** edit box which can used to define category of the shape. You can specify multiple keywords separated by **,** in the **Tags** edit box to create multiple tags.
*   Select desired toggle button from the **Shapes Settings** section in the window to define whether you want to create solid feature or hole feature.

- Select the **Lock part size (prevent scale)** check box to restrict changing of shape by scale tool in 3D Design workspace.
- After setting desired parameters, click on the **Save Shape** button from the window. The shape will be saved in **Your Creations** library of **Shapes** panel in **3D Design** workspace; refer to Figure-6.

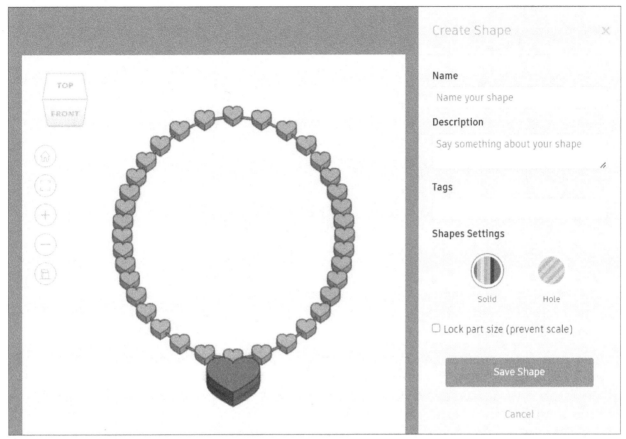

Figure-5. Create Shape window

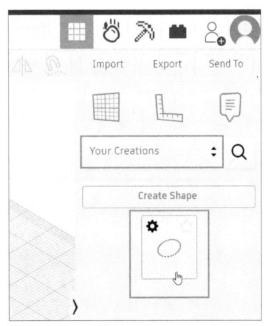

Figure-6. Shape added in Your Creations library

Sharing Screenshot and Animated GIF

The **Share** tool is used to share screenshot and animated gif of current codeblocks model. The procedure to use this tool is given next.

- Click on the **Share** tool from the toolbar. The **Sharing your creation** window will be displayed; refer to Figure-7.

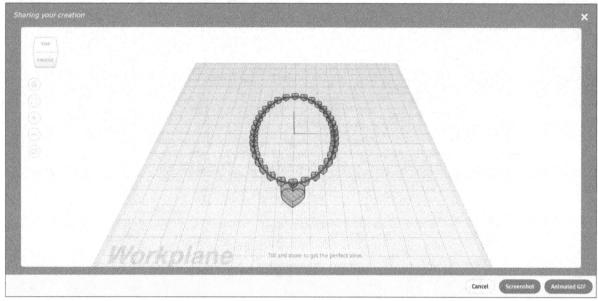

Figure-7. Sharing your creation window

- Click on the **Screenshot** button from the window to save current model display as a PNG image file. On doing so, PNG file will be downloaded.
- Click on the **Animated GIF** button from bottom right corner in the window to create an animated GIF image file. On clicking this button, system will execute the codeblocks and record them as a gif file. If you have created a complex codeblocks model then it may take some time for packaging. Once the packing is done, a GIF file will download in your system.
- Click on the **X** button at top right corner to close the window.

Blocks Panel

The objects in **Blocks** panel are called codeblocks; refer to Figure-8. These blocks can take inputs and generate output objects/operations. For example, **Box** block can be used to create a cube or cuboid with specified size parameters. You can scroll up/down in this panel to find desired codeblocks

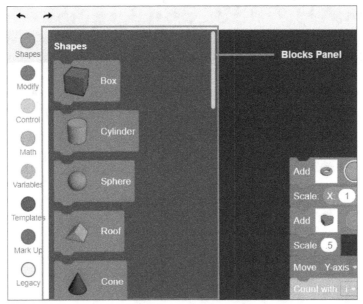

Figure-8. Blocks panel

Blocks Editor

The **Blocks Editor** panel of user interface is used to edit, connect, and manipulate blocks for creating 3D model; refer to Figure-9.

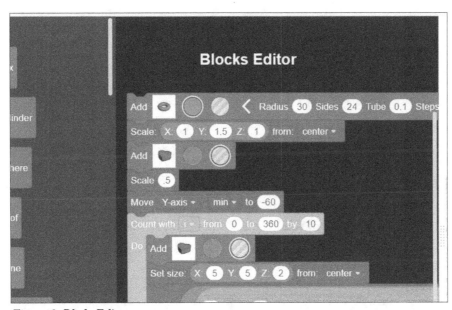

Figure-9. Blocks Editor

3D Viewer

The **3D Viewer** section available at the right in the user interface with work plane is used to check the model generated by codeblocks. You can use the ViewCube and common View orientation tools like Home, Zoom, Fit screen etc. to check the model in different view orientations.

USING CODEBLOCKS TEMPLATES

By default, there are some starter designs available in Tinkercad that can be used as template to create designs. The procedure to use these templates is given next.

- Click on the **Codeblocks** button at top left corner of application window to access various templates for starting design. The **Designs** dialog box will be displayed; refer to Figure-10.

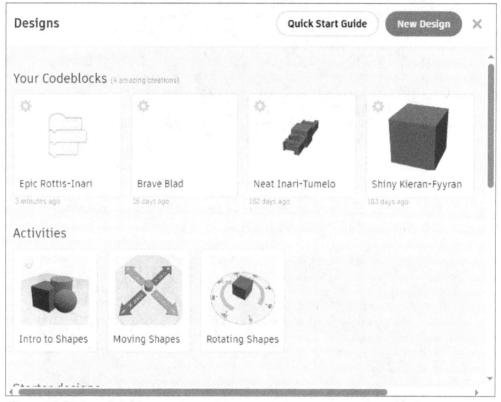

Figure-10. Designs dialog box

- Double-click on desired starter design to use it as template. A copy of selected design will be created and opened in the application window.
- Click on the **Quick Start Guide** button to check a basic help blog on functioning of codeblocks. You will be redirected to the **Tinkercad Resources** page in your web browser; refer to Figure-11.
- Click on the ☒ button to close the **Designs** dialog box.

Figure-11. Codeblocks quick start guide page

You can also start a new design by clicking on the **New Design** button from the **Designs** dialog box.

BLOCKS IN SHAPES LIBRARY

The blocks in the **Shapes** library are used to place various shapes like cylinder, box, roof, and so on in the model. Click on the **Shapes** tool from the left toolbar. The **Shapes** library will be displayed in **Blocks** panel; refer to Figure-12.

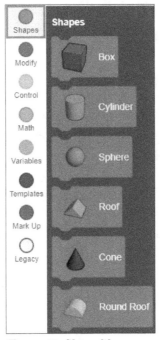

Figure-12. Shapes library

Placing Box

- Click on the **Box** tool from **Shapes** library and drag it to the **Block Editor** panel. The box block will be displayed in the **Block Editor** panel as shown in Figure-13.

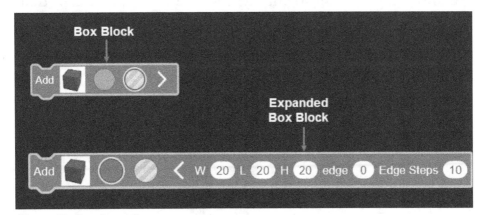

Figure-13. Box shape editor

- Click on the expand button ⟩ on the block to expand it and vice-versa. The expanded box block will be displayed; refer to Figure-13.
- Specify desired parameters in the edit boxes of the block to change its shape and size.

- After specifying the parameters, click on the **Run** button ▶ from the toolbar. The shape will be generated and displayed in the **3D Viewer** section of application window; refer to Figure-14.

Note: Every time you modify the parameters in the **Block Editor** panel or add new shape to the existing model then you need to re-run the entire block program using the **Run** button ▶ to reflect the modification.

Note: Blocks are executed based on their order in **Blocks Editor** panel from top to bottom. So, if you have placed a Cylinder block earlier in the Blocks panel and then place a Box block above it then box will be created first and after that cylinder will be created.

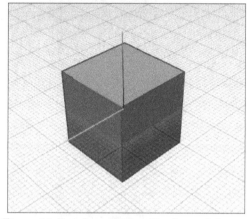

Figure-14. Box shape displayed in the workplane

Similarly, you can place the other blocks of the **Shapes** library in the **Blocks Editor** panel.

BLOCKS IN MODIFY LIBRARY

The blocks in **Modify** library are used to perform modifications on earlier placed blocks. For example, if you want to change the size of a box created using Box block then you will attach **Set size** block to that Box block and specify size modification parameters. Click on the **Modify** tool from the toolbar. The **Modify** library will be displayed; refer to Figure-15. Various blocks of this library are discussed next.

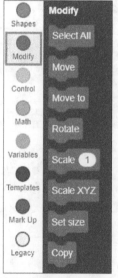

Figure-15. Modify library

Select All

The **Select All** block is used to select the object created by blocks before this block in **Blocks Editor** panel. Click & hold the **Select All** block and drag it to the block panel below the existing block; refer to Figure-16. On executing the codeblocks, all the objects placed before this block will get selected.

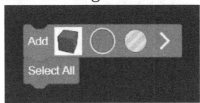

Figure-16. Select All block placed

Move

The **Move** block is used to move the shape above this block at specified coordinates. The procedure to use this block is given next.

- Click and drag the **Move** block to the **Block Editor** panel below an existing block to move it; refer to Figure-17.
- Specify desired value in the **X**, **Y**, or **Z** edit boxes to move the shape along x axis, y axis, or z axis by specified amount.

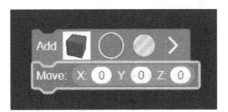

Figure-17. Move tool placed

Move to

The **Move to** block is used to move attached shape by specified distance along selected axis. The procedure to use this block is given next.

- Click and drag the **Move to** block below the existing block in **Block Editor** panel; refer to Figure-18.

Figure-18. Move to block placed

- Select desired axis from drop-down in the block along which the shape is to be moved.
- Specify desired distance by which the shape is to be moved in the **to** edit box.
- Select the **max** option from the drop-down if you want to use the point of object at maximum distance along selected axis from the origin as reference and move it by specified value. Select the **min** option to use point at minimum distance from origin along selected axis as reference point for moving. Similarly, select the **center** option from the drop-down to use center of object as reference; refer to Figure-19. After specifying desired parameters, click on the ▶ button. The shape will be moved.

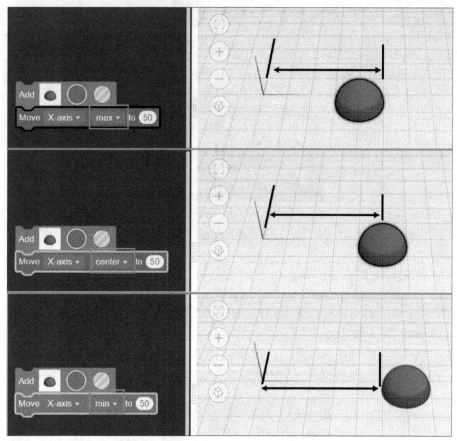

Figure-19. Setting reference for move

Rotate

The **Rotate** block is used to rotate the attached block shape by specified angle. The procedure to use this block is given next.

- Click and drag the **Rotate** block to the **Block Editor** panel below the existing block to be rotated; refer to Figure-20.

Figure-20. Rotate block placed

- Select desired option from **around** drop-down in block to define the axis about which object will be rotated. By default, red colored axis in graphics area is X-axis, green colored axis is Y-axis, and blue colored axis is Z-axis; refer to Figure-21.
- Specify desired angle value in **by** edit box to define angle by which object will be rotated.
- By default, object rotates about its own axes using its center point as origin when you have not specified value in the **Pivot** input box of codeblock; refer to Figure-22.
- Drag the **Vector3** block from **Math** library and place it in **Pivot** input box to define coordinates of pivot point; refer to Figure-23. By default, 0,0,0 values are set in the **Vector3** block which represent the origin of workplane. So, if we run the program now then object will rotate about the origin of workplane and not about its own origin; refer to Figure-24.

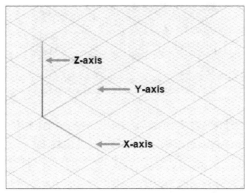

Figure-21. Axes in graphics area

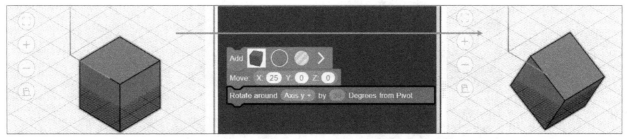

Figure-22. When rotating without pivot

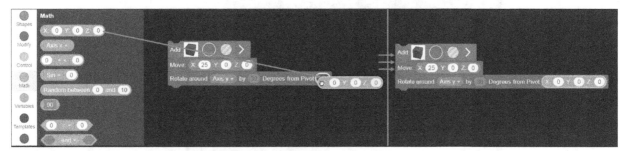

Figure-23. Inserting Vector3 code in Pivot input

Figure-24. Object rotating about workplane origin

Scale

The **Scale** block is used to increase or decrease the size of attached block by specified scale factor. The procedure to use this block is given next.

- Click and drag the **Scale** block to the **Block Editor** panel below the existing block to be scaled; refer to Figure-25.

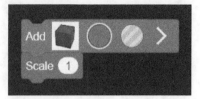

Figure-25. Scale block placed

• Specify desired value in the edit box of the **Scale** block to define factor for scaling. For example, if you specify the value as **2** then object size will double; refer to Figure-26. Similarly, you specify the value as **0.5** then object size will half.

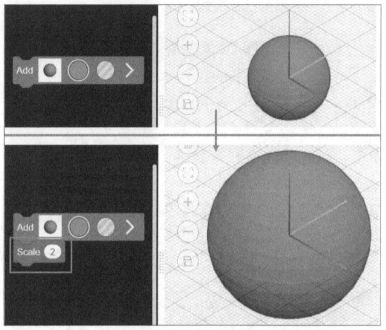

Figure-26. Applying scale

Scale XYZ

The **Scale XYZ** block is used to scale the shape individually along x, y, and z axes. The procedure to use this block is given next.

• Click and drag the **Scale XYZ** block to the **Blocks Editor** panel below the existing block to be scaled; refer to Figure-27.

Figure-27. Scale XYZ block placed

• Specify desired value in the **X**, **Y**, and **Z** edit boxes to scale the shape along x, y, and z axis, respectively.
• Select desired option in the **from** drop-down to define reference point to be used for scaling. After specifying desired parameters, click on the ▶ button. The shape will be scaled; refer to Figure-28.

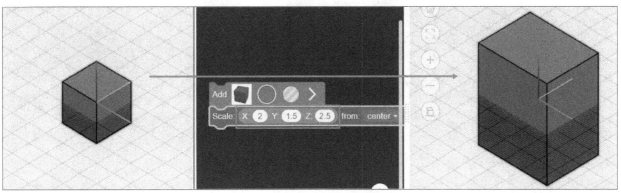

Figure-28. Shape scaled along axis

Set Size

The **Set Size** block is used to set desired size of shape along X, Y, and Z axes using an imaginary bounding box. The procedure to use this tool is same as discussed for previous tool.

Copy

The **Copy** block is used to create a copy the attached shape at its location. The procedure to use this tool is given next.

- Click and drag the **Copy** block to the **Blocks Editor** panel below the existing block to be copied; refer to Figure-29.

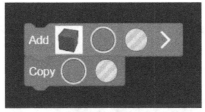

Figure-29. Copy block placed

- Set desired solid color or hole settings for the shape as discussed earlier.

Similarly, you can use the **Set color**, **Set color RGB**, and **Set color HSB** blocks as discussed earlier in **3D Design** workspace to set desired color of attached object using color palette, RGB values, and HSB values, respectively.

Create Group

The **Create Group** block is used to combine all the shapes that have been placed before it in the **Blocks Editor** panel. This block functions similar to **Group** tool in 3D Design workspace.

Position

The **Position** block is used to store the value of minimum, maximum, or center point of the object to which this block is attached. This block is placed in Input box of other blocks to provide a value. Take the following case as an example to understand the functioning. Assume that you have a box of size 30x45x10 in WxLxH format. You want to rotate this box about its own axis by value equal to distance of maximum point of this box from origin along Y-axis which comes out to be 22.5 in this case. Then Figure-30 shows the code blocks for this operation.

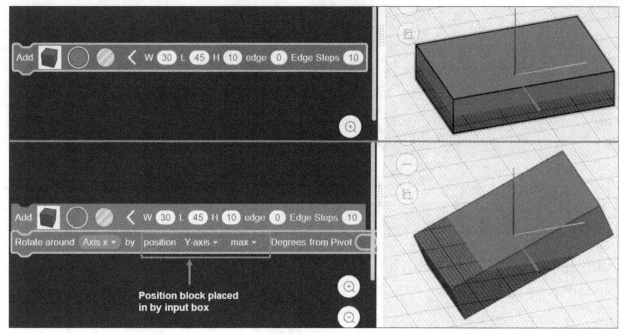

Figure-30. Using position block

Size Block

The **Size** block is used to store size of attached object along selected axis and this block can be inserted in the input box of the other blocks for output stored value. If we take the same example as discussed earlier for **Position** block and place **Size** block in place of **Position** block in the **Rotate** block then the same object will rotate by 45 degree which is the size of box along Y axis; refer to Figure-31.

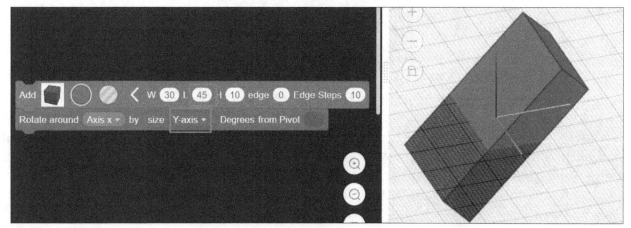

Figure-31. Using size block

BLOCKS IN CONTROL LIBRARY

Click on the **Control** tool from the toolbar at the left in application window. The **Control** library will be displayed; refer to Figure-32. The blocks in this library are used to perform operations like repeating execution of blocks, setting conditions for execution of blocks, and so on. Various blocks of this library are discussed next.

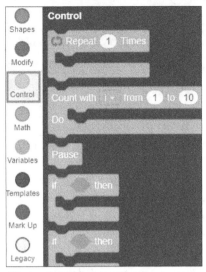

Figure-32. Control workspace

Repeat Block

The **Repeat** block is used to repeat execution of blocks inside its range by specified number of times. The procedure to use this block is given next.

- Click on the **Repeat** block and drag it to the **Blocks Editor** panel; refer to Figure-33.

Figure-33. Repeat tool

- Specify desired number of times in the repeat edit box to repeat execution of block codes inside this block. For example, in Figure-34 we have created a linear pattern of box by repeating creation and moving of block 5 times.

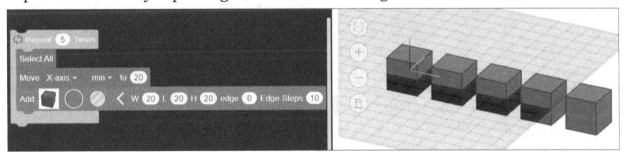

Figure-34. Repeat block example

Count-Do Block (For Loop)

The **Count-Do** block is used when you want to use value change of a variable as reference for repeating some tasks. For example, if we set **i** variable to count from 1 to 10 with increment of 1 and put some block codes in the **Count-Do** block then execution of block codes will be performed 10 times. The procedure to use this block is given next.

- Click and drag the **Count-Do** block from **Control** library to **Blocks Editor** panel; refer to Figure-35.

Figure-35. Count-Do block

- Select desired option from the **with** drop-down to define variable to be used for running loop. (Loop is repetition of a task till certain conditions are being fulfilled.) By default, **i** is used in this drop-down. You will learn to create new variables later in this chapter.
- Specify desired value in the **from** edit box to define starting point for loop condition.
- Specify desired value in the **to** edit box to define the end point for loop condition.
- Specify desired value in the **by** edit box to define the increment by which starting value of variable will change on executing codes in the **Count-Do** block.
- Now, drag other code blocks inside this block to perform loop execution. We can use the previous linear pattern example discussed in **Repeat** block and put it in **Count-Do** block to create rectangular pattern; refer to Figure-36.

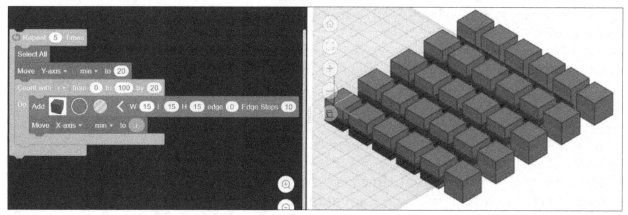

Figure-36. Count-Do example rectangular pattern

Pause Block

The **Pause** block is used to pause execution of current program until you click on the ▶ button again. Drag the block and place it in **Blocks Editor** panel after desired block to pause program execution; refer to Figure-37. In the shown figure, on execution of program, system will create a box and pause. After you click on **Play** button again then roof object will be created in **3D Viewer**.

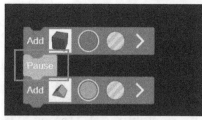

Figure-37. Pause block example

If-Then Block

The **If-Then** block is used when you want to perform execution of code blocks on when a certain condition is met. For example, you want to create a box of 30x30x20 if value of i variable is equal to 10. The procedure to use this block is given next.

- Click and drag the **If-Then** block from the **Control** library to the **Blocks Editor** panel. The block will be placed; refer to Figure-38.

Figure-38. If-Then block

- Specify desired condition block in the **if** input box to be define condition of block.
- Place the code blocks inside the **If-Then** block that are to be executed if the condition of the block is met. For example, if you want to change color of one block which is at distance of 60 mm from origin in each linear pattern to green in previous example then you can use the **If-Then** block as shown in Figure-39.

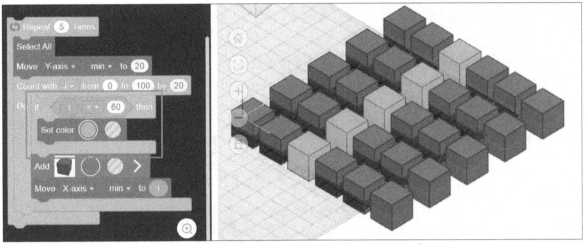

Figure-39. Using If-Then block

If-Then-Else Block

The **If-Then-Else** block is used to execute either of the two different code blocks based on answer of If condition. The procedure to use this block is given next.

- Click and drag the **If-Then-Else** block from the **Control** library to the **Blocks Editor** panel. The block will be placed; refer to Figure-40.

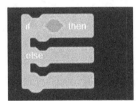

Figure-40. If-else-then block

- Place the condition block in **if** input box of code block and similarly, place the other blocks to be executed based on if condition as discussed earlier. If we take the previous example and want to increase the size of all red blocks to 1.25 times while leaving the green blocks unchanged then we can use the **If-Else-Then** code block as shown in Figure-41.

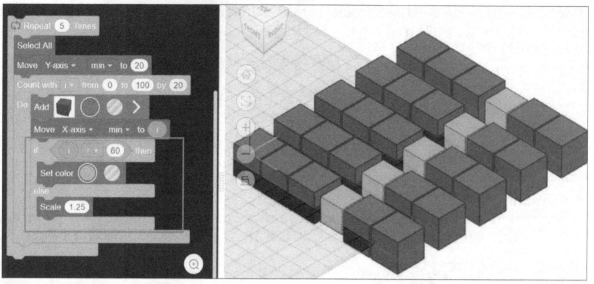

Figure-41. Using If-else-then code block

MATH TAB

The blocks in **Math** library of **Blocks** panel are used to insert mathematical equations and variables in the code block design. Click on the **Math** tool from the toolbar at the left in the application window to display the **Math** library; refer to Figure-42. Various blocks of this library are discussed next.

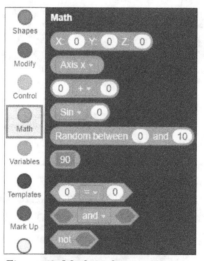

Figure-42. Math workspace

Vector3 Block

The **Vector3** block is used as an output vector block which takes values of X, Y, and Z coordinates as input. You can use this block as input for other blocks where you need to specify position vector for the point. The procedure to use this block is given next.

- Click and drag the **Vector 3** block from **Math** library to **Blocks Editor** panel. The block will be displayed as shown in Figure-43.

Figure-43. Vector3 block

- Click in the **X** edit box of block to specify coordinate along X axis. Similarly, specify coordinates along Y and Z axes in respective edit boxes of the block.
- You can drag this block in input field of other blocks which need position vector like **Rotate** block; refer to Figure-44.

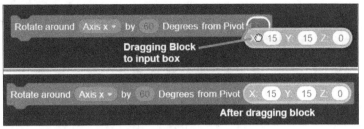

Figure-44. Using Vector3 block in Rotate block

Axis Block

The **Axis** block of **Math** library is used as axis direction input box for other blocks which require axis direction as input. The procedure to use this block is given next.

- Drag the **Axis** block from the **Math** library into **Blocks Editor** panel. The block will be displayed as shown in Figure-45.

Figure-45. Axis block

- Select desired axis direction option from the drop-down in the block.
- Drag this block in axis input box of other blocks to use the block as input.

Arithmetic Operation Block

The **Arithmetic Operation** block is used to perform arithmetic operation two specified values/variables and output the result. The procedure to use this block is given next.

- Drag the **Arithmetic Operation** block from the **Math** library in **Blocks Editor** panel. The block will be displayed as shown in Figure-46.

Figure-46. Arithmetic block

- Select desired mathematical operator like plus (**+**), minus (**-**), multiply (*****), or divide (**/**) from the drop-down in the block to perform respective operation. Select the **mod** operator to find out remainder on dividing left side value in the block by right side value. Select the **pow** operator from the drop-down if you want to use **x**^{y} equation where **x** is the left side value in the block and **y** is the right side value in the block.
- Specify desired values in the edit boxes. You can also drag variable blocks in these input edit boxes to use them in mathematical operation. You will learn about variables later.

Math Function Block

The Math function block is used to create various mathematical expression like Sin, Cos, Tan, Absolute of, Round, Square Root, Log2, Log, and so on. The procedure to use this block is given next.

- Click and drag the **Math function** block from the **Math** library to **Blocks Editor** panel. The block will be displayed as shown in Figure-47.

Figure-47. Math function block

- Select desired option from drop-down in the block and set desired value in the edit box. The output of this block can be used as input for other blocks.

Random Block

The **Random** block is used to provide random number as output from specified range. The procedure to use this block is given next.

- Click and drag the **Random** block from the **Math** library to **Blocks Editor** panel. The block will be displayed as shown in Figure-48.

Figure-48. Random block

- Specify desired values in the **between** and **and** edit boxes of the block to define range from which a random number will be chosen. This block is also used as input for other blocks.

Input Degrees Block

The **Input Degrees** block is used when you want to provide angle value in mathematical functions. The procedure to use this tool is given next.

- Click and drag the **Input Degrees** block from the **Math** library to **Blocks Editor** panel. The block will be displayed as shown in Figure-49.
- Click in the edit box of block. A clock handle will be displayed to graphically set the angle value; refer to Figure-50. You can also type the value in edit box.

Figure-49. Input Degrees block

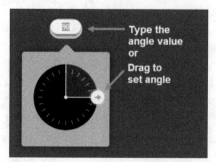

Figure-50. Specifying input angle

Condition Operator Block

The **Condition Operator** block is used to output true or false as output based on condition parameters defined in the block. You can use equal (=), not equal(≠), greater than(>), greater than or equal to (≥), less than (<), and less than or equal to (≤) as condition operators in the block. The procedure to use this block is given next.

- Click and drag the **Condition Operator** block from the **Math** library to **Blocks Editor** panel. The block will be displayed as shown in Figure-51.

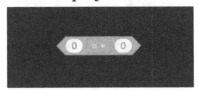

Figure-51. Condition operator block

- Set desired operator in the drop-down of this block and set the parameters as discussed earlier.

And-Or Block

The **And-or** block is used to define whether you want to output a true value when **and** condition is true or when the **or** condition is true. The procedure to use this block is given next.

- Click and drag the **And-or** block from the **Math** library to **Blocks Editor** panel. The block will be displayed as shown in Figure-52.

Figure-52. And-or block

- Set desired condition operator blocks in the input boxes of the block.
- Select the **and** option from the drop-down if you want to output true value when conditions of both input boxes are true. Select the **or** option from drop-down if you want to output true value when condition of any one of the two input boxes is true. For example, in Figure-53 the block with **and** operator will give False as output because left size condition in the block is not true and for **and** operator to give True value as output, both conditions must be true. Although, block with **or** operator will give True as output because one of the two conditions is correct.

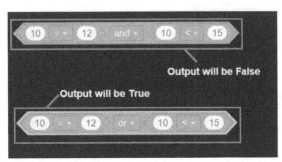

Figure-53. Use of And-or block

Not Block

The **Not** block is used to flip the output of other Condition blocks that output True or False value. The procedure to use this block is given next.

*   Click and drag the **Not** block from the **Math** library to **Blocks Editor** panel. The block will be displayed as shown in Figure-54.

Figure-54. Not block

*   Put the condition operator in the input field which you want to be not true. For example, if you put the block with or operator discussed in previous topic as input then it will output False value; refer to Figure-55.

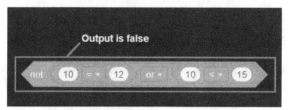

Figure-55. Using Not block

VARIABLES TAB

Click on the **Variables** tool from the toolbar at the left in application window. The **Variables** library will be displayed; refer to Figure-56. The blocks in this library are used to create and place variables for performing other operations. Variables act as container for number or other parameters. These variables can be used in algebraic equations to create unique mathematical shapes. Various blocks of this library are discussed next.

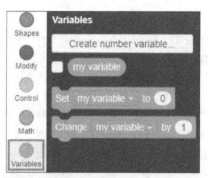

Figure-56. Variables library

Creating Number Variables

The **Create Number Variables** button in **Variables** library is used to create new variables. The procedure to create number variable is given next.

*   Click on the **Create Number Variables** button from the **Variables** library of **Block** panel. An input box will be displayed to specify name of the variable; refer to Figure-57.

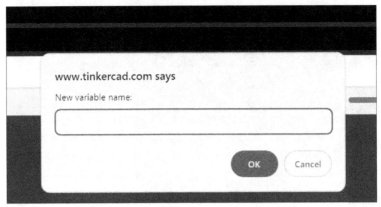

Figure-57. Input box for variable name

- Specify desired name in the input box and click **OK** to create the variable. The variable will be created and added below the **Create number variable** button; refer to Figure-58. Generally, single alphabets are used for naming variables.

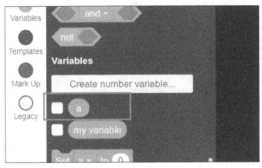

Figure-58. New variable created

- After creating variable, you can assign values to it and you can use it for algebraic solutions; refer to Figure-59.

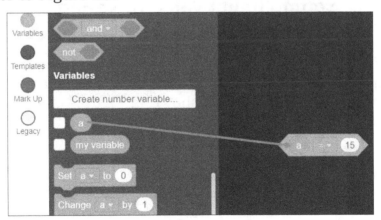

Figure-59. Assigning value to variable

- Select check box available before the variable name in the **Variables** library if you want to check value of variable during the execution of code blocks; refer to Figure-60.

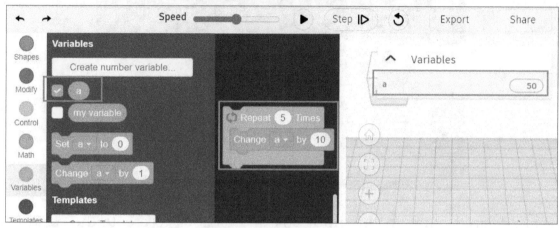

Figure-60. Showing variable value in 3D Viewer

- If you want to delete a variable then right-click on it in the **Variables** library and select the **Delete the ' ' variable** option from the shortcut menu; refer to Figure-61.

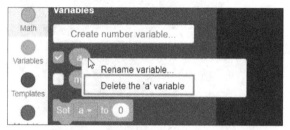

Figure-61. Deleting variable

Setting Initial Value of Variable

The **Set-to** block is used to set initial value of a variable. The procedure to use this block is given next.

- Click and drag the **Set-to** block from the **Variables** library to **Blocks Editor** panel. The block will be displayed as shown in Figure-62.

Figure-62. Set-to block

- Click on the **Set** drop-down in the block to select desired variable. The options will be displayed as shown in Figure-63.

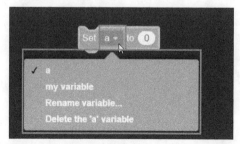

Figure-63. Set drop-down

- Select desired variable from the **Set** drop-down to be assigned in the block.
- Select the **Rename variable** option from the **Set** drop-down to change name of current selected variable.
- Specify desired value in the **to** edit box to be set for the variable.

Change-by

The **Change-by** block is used to change value of variable by specified amount. You can use this block to increase as well as decrease the value of variable. The procedure to use this block is given next.

- Click and drag the **Change-by** block from the **Variables** library to **Blocks Editor** panel. The block will be displayed as shown in Figure-64.

Figure-64. Change by block

- Select desired variable from the drop-down in block to be changed.
- Specify desired value in the **by** edit box to define amount by which value of variable will change. Specify positive value to increase variable's value and negative value to decrease variable's value.

TEMPLATES TAB

Click on the **Templates** tool from the toolbar, the **Templates** library will be displayed; refer to Figure-65. The blocks in this library are used to create and manage template blocks. The blocks of this library are discussed next.

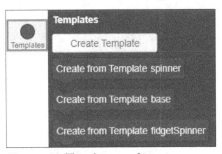

Figure-65. Templates workspace

Creating Template

The **Create Template** button is used to generate two blocks; one for defining template and other for creating object using earlier defined template. The procedure to create template is given next.

- Click on the **Create Template** button from the **Template** library. An input box will be displayed asking for name of the template; refer to Figure-66.

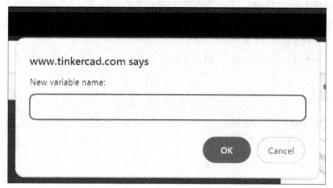

Figure-66. Input box for template name

- Specify desired name in the input box and click on the **OK** button. The **Define Template** and **Create from Template** blocks with specified name will be placed in the **Blocks Editor** panel.
- Add desired blocks in the **Define Template** block to define the shape/design of template block. After defining template, place the **Create from Template** block in loops/conditions wherever you want to create object using template; refer to Figure-67.

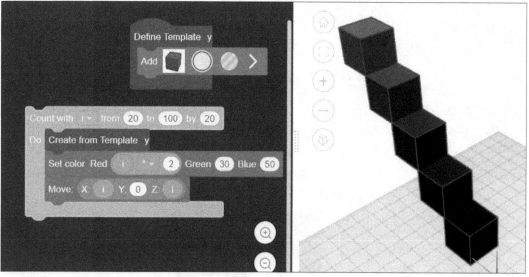

Figure-67. Using template

Note that you need to delete the **Create from Template** block first before deleting the **Define Template** block.

MARK UP TAB

Click on the **Mark Up** tool from the toolbar, the **Mark up** library will be displayed; refer to Figure-68. The blocks in this library are used to add comments about programming blocks or display messages in the 3D Viewer when running program. The blocks of this library are discussed next.

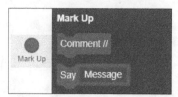

Figure-68. Mark up workspace

Comment

The **Comment** block is used to add comments about the code block in the **Blocks Editor** panel. Generally, this block is used as hint about what a section of blocks does so that later we can find the problem section fast if program does not work as intended. The procedure to use this block is given next.

- Click and drag the **Comment** block from the **Mark Up** library to **Blocks Editor** panel. The block will be displayed as shown in Figure-69.

Figure-69. Comment block

- Specify desired comment in the comment box and attach it to the blocks as needed. Note that these comments will not be displayed in the **3D Viewer** on running program.

Say

The **Say** block is used to add comments in the program that will be displayed in the **3D Viewer** when running the codeblocks. The procedure to use this block is given next.

- Click and drag the **Say** block from the **Mark Up** library to **Blocks Editor** panel. The block will be displayed as shown in Figure-70.

Figure-70. Say block

- Specify desired text in the **Message** box. To display the message on the **3D Viewer**, click on the **Play** button from the toolbar; refer to Figure-71.

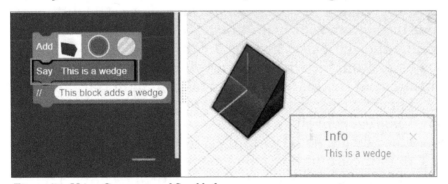

Figure-71. Using Comment and Say blocks

LEGACY TAB

Click on the **Legacy** tab from the toolbar, the **Legacy** library will be displayed; refer to Figure-72. The blocks in this library do the same job as discussed for **Template** blocks. So, these blocks will be removed from software soon.

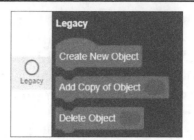

Figure-72. Legacy workspace

PRACTICAL 1

Create the 3D design using codeblocks; refer to Figure-73.

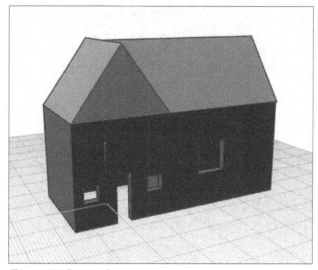

Figure-73. Practical 1

- Start a new Codeblocks design.
- Click & hold the **Box** block from the **Shapes** library and drag it to the **Blocks Editor** panel. The **Box** block will be displayed. Expand the box and specify the width, length, and height of box as **30** in the **W**, **L**, and **H** edit boxes, respectively.
- Drag the **Move** block from **Modify** library and connect it below the Box block earlier created. Specify the value as **15** in the **Z** edit box.
- Drag the **Box** block from the **Shapes** library and connect it to previous block. Select the **Hole** button from the block to convert it into material removing box. Expand the block and specify the width, length, and height as **26**, **26**, and **32** in the **W**, **L**, and **H** edit boxes, respectively.
- Drag the **Move** block from **Modify** library and connect it to previous block. Specify the value as **15** in the **Z** edit box.
- Drag the **Select All** block from the **Modify** library and connect it to previous block.
- Drag the **Create Group** block from the **Modify** library and connect it to previous block.
- Drag the **Roof** block from the **Shapes** library and connect it to previous block. Specify the length as **20** in the **L** edit box.
- Drag the **Set Size** block from the **Modify** library and connect it to previous block. Specify the value of **X**, **Y**, and **Z** as **30**, **30**, and **20** from the center, respectively.
- Drag the **Move** block from **Modify** library and connect it to previous block. Specify the value along Z axis as **45** in the **Z** edit box.
- Drag the **Box** block from the **Shapes** library and connect it to previous block. Select the **Hole** button from the block. Expand the block and specify the width, length, and height as **5**, **5**, and **15** in the **W**, **L**, and **H** edit boxes, respectively.

- Drag the **Move** block from **Modify** library and connect it to previous block. Specify the values along Y and Z axes as **15** and **7** in the **Y** and **Z** edit boxes, respectively.
- Drag the **Select All** block from the **Modify** library and connect it to previous block.
- Drag the **Create Group** block from the **Modify** library and connect it to previous block.
- Drag the **Box** block from the **Shapes** library and connect it to previous block. Specify the width, length, and height as **40, 30,** and **30** in the **W, L,** and **H** edit boxes, respectively.
- Drag the **Move** block from **Modify** library and connect it to previous block. Specify the values along X and Z axes as **-35** and **15** in the **X** and **Z** edit boxes, respectively.
- Drag the **Select All** block from the **Modify** library and connect it to previous block.
- Drag the **Create Group** block from the **Modify** library and connect it to previous block.
- Drag the **Roof** block from the **Shapes** library and connect it to previous block. Specify the length as **20** in the **L** edit box.
- Drag the **Move** block from **Modify** library and connect it to previous block. Specify the values along X and Z axes as **-28** and **40** in the **X** and **Z** edit boxes, respectively.
- Drag the **Rotate** block from the **Modify** library and connect it to previous block. Specify the value of rotation as **90⁰** from the **Z** axis.
- Drag the **Set Size** block from the **Modify** library and connect it to previous block. Specify the value of **X, Y,** and **Z** as **55, 30,** and **20** from the center, respectively.
- Drag the **Box** block from the **Shapes** library and connect it to previous block. Select the **Hole** button from the block. Expand the block and specify the width, length, and height as **10, 5,** and **10** in the **W, L,** and **H** edit boxes, respectively.
- Drag the **Move** block from **Modify** library and connect it to previous block. Specify the values along X, Y, and Z axes as **-30, 15,** and **15** in the **X, Y,** and **Z** edit boxes, respectively.
- Drag the **Select All** block from the **Modify** library and connect it to previous block.
- Drag the **Create Group** block from the **Modify** library and connect it to previous block.
- Drag the **Box** block from the **Shapes** library and connect it to previous block. Select the **Hole** button from the block. Expand the block and specify the width, length, and height as **5, 5,** and **5** in the **W, L,** and **H** edit boxes, respectively.
- Drag the **Move** block from **Modify** library and connect it to previous block. Specify the values along x, y, and z axes as **10, 15,** and **10** in the **X, Y,** and **Z** edit boxes, respectively.
- Drag the **Select All** block from the **Modify** library and connect it to previous block.
- Drag the **Create Group** block from the **Modify** library and connect it to previous block.
- Drag the **Box** block from the **Shapes** library and connect it to previous block. Select the **Hole** button from the block. Expand the block and specify the width, length, and height as **5, 5,** and **5** in the **W, L,** and **H** edit boxes, respectively.
- Drag the **Move** block from **Modify** library and connect it to previous block. Specify the values along x, y, and z axis as **-10, 15,** and **10** in the **X, Y,** and **Z** edit boxes, respectively.
- Drag the **Select All** block from the **Modify** library and connect it to previous block.
- Drag the **Create Group** block from the **Modify** library and connect it to previous block.
- After specifying all the parameters, click on the ▶ button from the toolbar. The 3D Design will be created; refer to Figure-74.

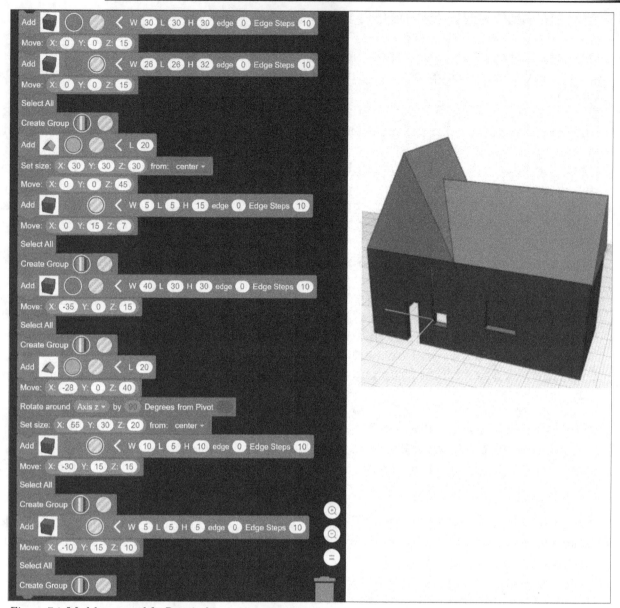

Figure-74. Model generated for Practical 1

PRACTICAL 2

Create a Rocket in CodeBlock 3D Practical; refer to Figure-75.

Figure-75. Practical 2

- Start a new Codeblocks design.
- Click and drag the **Cylinder** block from the **Shapes** library to the **Blocks Editor** panel. Expand the block and specify the **Radius**, **Height**, and **Sides** as **10**, **100**, and **20**, respectively.
- Drag the **Move** block from **Modify** library and connect it to previous block. Specify the value along Z axis as **50** in the **Z** edit box.
- Drag the **Cylinder** block from the **Shapes** library and connect it to previous block. Specify the **Radius**, **Height** and **Sides** as **10**, **60**, and **20**, respectively.
- Drag the **Move** block from the **Modify** library and connect it to previous block. Specify the values along X and Z axes as **20** and **40** in the **X** and **Z** edit boxes, respectively.
- Drag the **Copy** block from the **Modify** library and connect it to previous block.
- Drag the **Move** block from **Modify** library and connect it to previous block. Specify the value along X axis as **-40** in the **X** edit box.
- Drag the **Paraboloid** block from the **Shapes** library and connect it to previous block. Specify the **Radius** and **Height** as **10** and **20**, respectively.
- Drag the **Move** block from **Modify** library and connect it to previous block. Specify the value along Z axis as **110** in the **Z** edit box.
- Drag the **Paraboloid** block from the **Shapes** library and connect it to previous block. Specify the **Radius** and **Height** as **10** and **20**, respectively.
- Drag the **Move** block from the **Modify** library and connect it to previous block. Specify the values along X and Z axes as **-20** and **80** in the **X** and **Z** edit boxes, respectively.
- Drag the **Copy** block from the **Modify** library and connect it to previous block.
- Drag the **Move** block from **Modify** library and connect it to previous block. Specify the value along X axis as **40** in the **X** edit box.
- Drag the **Star** button from the **Shapes** library and connect it to previous block. Specify the **Sides** and **Radius** as **5** and **20**, respectively.
- Drag the **Move** block from **Modify** library and connect it to previous block. Specify the value along X axis as **2** in the **X** edit box.

- Drag the **Text** block from the **Shapes** library and connect it to previous block. Specify the text as shown in Figure-32 in the text box and specify the height of text as **10** in the **H** edit box.
- Drag the **Set Size** block from the **Modify** library and connect it to previous block. Specify the values of **X**, **Y**, and **Z** as **50, 5,** and **2** from the center, respectively.
- Drag the **Move** block from **Modify** library and connect it to previous block. Specify the value along Y axis as **-20** in the **Y** edit box.
- Drag the **Rotate** block from the **Modify** library and connect it to previous block. Specify the value of rotation as **90⁰** from the **X-axis**.
- Drag the **Move** block from **Modify** library and connect it to previous block. Specify the value of y and z axis as **10** and **50** in the **Y** and **Z** edit boxes, respectively.
- Drag the **Rotate** block from the **Modify** library and connect it to previous block. Specify the value of rotation as **90⁰** from the **Y** axis.
- Drag the **Select All** block from the **Modify** library and connect it to previous block.
- Drag the **Move** block from **Modify** library and connect it to previous block. Specify the value along Z axis as **10** in the **Z** edit box.
- Drag the **Move** block from **Modify** library and connect it to previous block. Specify the value along Z axis as **200** in the **Z** edit box.
- After specifying all the parameters, click on the ▶ button from the toolbar. The 3D Design will be created; refer to Figure-76.

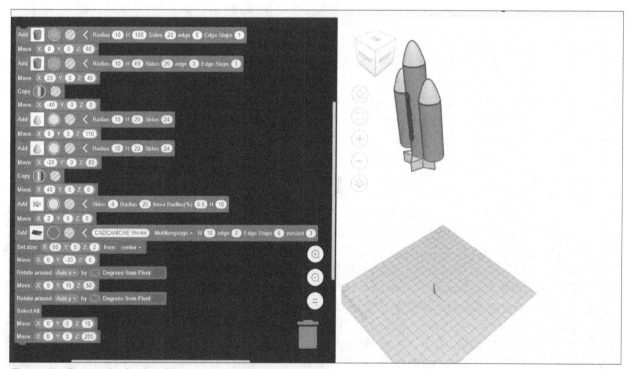

Figure-76. Practical 2 final model

PRACTICAL 3

Create a clock using code blocks as shown in Figure-77.

Figure-77. Practical 3

- Start a new Codeblocks design.
- Drag the **Cylinder** block from the **Shapes** section and specify the **Radius**, **Height**, and **Sides** as **30**, **3**, and **50**, respectively.
- Drag the **Move** block from **Modify** library and connect it to previous block. Specify the value of Z axis as **2** in the **Z** edit box.
- Drag the **Cylinder** block from the **Shapes** section and connect it to previous block. Select the **Hole** button from block and specify the **Radius**, **Height**, and **Sides** as **28**, **10**, and **50**, respectively.
- Drag the **Move** block from **Modify** library and connect it to previous block. Specify the value along Z axis as **7** in the **Z** edit box.
- Drag the **Select All** block and then **Create Group** block from the **Modify** library and connect them to previous block.
- Drag and place the **Repeat** block connected to previous block. Set its repetition to **12**.
- Place **Box**, **Move**, and **Rotate** blocks inside the **Repeat** block and set the parameters as shown in Figure-78. Note that we have used '**i**' variable for applying rotation.

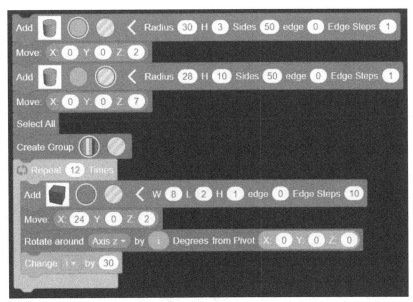

Figure-78. Setting parameters for Repeat block

- Drag the **Box** block from the **Shapes** section and connect it to previous block. Specify the **Width**, **Length**, and **Height** as **18**, **1.5**, and **1**, respectively.
- Drag the **Move** block from **Modify** library and connect it to previous block. Specify the values along X and Z axis as **9** and **5** in the **X** and **Z** edit boxes, respectively.
- Drag and place the **Repeat** block connected to previous block. Set its repetition to **200**.
- Drag the **Rotate** block from **Modify** library and connect it to previous block. Set the rotation about Axis Z by **-5** degree.
- Drag the **Vector3** block from **Math** library and place it in **Degrees from Pivot** input box of **Rotate** block placed earlier.
- After specifying all the parameters, click on the ▶ button from the toolbar. The 3D Design will be created; refer to Figure-79.

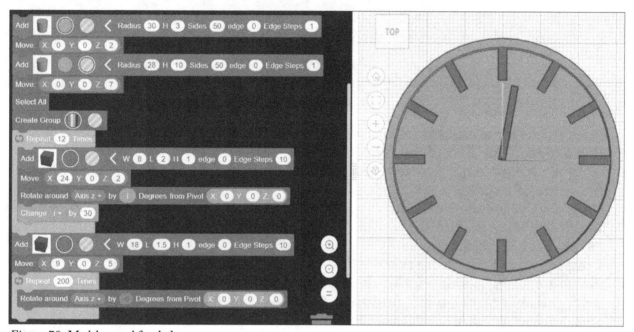

Figure-79. Model created for clock

PRACTICAL 4

Create a necklace of hearts patterned on an ellipse shape as shown in Figure-80.

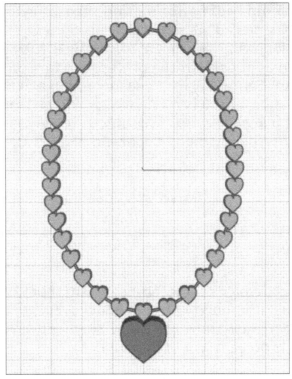

Figure-80. Practical 4

- Start a new Codeblocks design.
- Drag the **Torus** block from **Shapes** library to **Blocks Editor** panel and set **Radius** to **30**, **Sides** to **24**, **Tube** to **0.1**, and **Steps** to **25** values. This will create a circular tube on running codes.
- Drag the **Scale XYZ** block from the **Modify** library and connect it to previous block. Set the values **1**, **1.5**, and **1** from center in the **X**, **Y**, and **Z** edit boxes, respectively. This will convert the circular tube to an elliptical tube with major diameter 30 x 1.5 = **45** mm and minor diameter to **30** mm on running codes.
- Drag the **Heart** block from **Shapes** library to **Blocks Editor** panel and connect it to previous block. This will place a heart shape in 3D Viewer on running codes.
- Drag the **Scale** block from the **Modify** library and connect it to previous block. Set the value as **0.5** to reduce the size of heart to half.
- Drag the **Move to** block from the **Modify** library and connect it to previous block. Set the value as **-60** from **min** position along **Y-axis** to move the heart at the bottom center of ellipse.
- Drag the **Count-Do** block from the **Control** library and connect it to previous block. Set the parameters as **i** in the **with** drop-down, **0** in the **from** edit box, **360** in the **to** edit box and **10** in the **by** edit box of the block. This block will repeat whatever codes are put in it until value of **i** reaches from 0 to 360 and on each execution of codeblocks inside this block, value of **i** is increased by **10**. So, this code will repeat code blocks inside it **36** times.
- Drag **Heart** block inside the **Count-Do** block earlier created. Change the color of heart in the **Heart** block to light pink. This will create pink colored heart shapes.
- Drag the **Set size** block from **Modify** library and place it below the **Heart** block placed earlier inside **Count-Do** block. Set the parameters as **5**, **5**, **2** in the **X**, **Y**, and **Z** edit boxes from center in the block. This will reduce the size of heart shapes to be patterned along tube.

- Drag the **Move** block from **Modify** library and place it below previous block in the **Count-Do** block earlier placed. Since, we need to create multiple copies of small heart which will be following perimeter of elliptical tube for their placement, we will take help of mathematical formula of ellipse to find out X and Y coordinates of heart shapes; refer to Figure-81. In these formulas, **a** is the major axis diameter, **b** is minor axis diameter, and **θ** is angle which will go from 0 to 360 degrees. We will use **i** variable in place of **θ** when creating the code blocks of formula because, we are changing **i** variable by using **Count-Do** block.

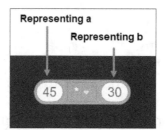

$$x = \frac{ab\cos(\theta)}{\sqrt{(a\sin(\theta))^2 + (b\cos(\theta))^2}}$$

$$y = \frac{ab\sin(\theta)}{\sqrt{(a\sin(\theta))^2 + (b\cos(\theta))^2}}$$

Figure-81. Elipse coordinates

- Now, we will create code block for **x**. Drag the **Arithmetic Operation** block from **Math** library and place it in empty area of **Blocks Editor** panel. Set the operator in block to multiply (*) and values to **45** and **30** in edit boxes of the block; refer to Figure-82. This will represent **axb** of formula.

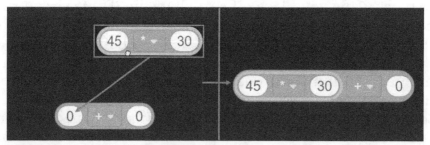

Figure-82. axb in blocks

- Place another **Arithmetic Operation** block in empty area of block and drag **axb** formula block in one input box of the block; refer to Figure-83.

Figure-83. Placing axb in other block

- Similarly, place other blocks and set values to create formula for X position as shown in Figure-84.

![Figure-84 formula blocks: 45 * 30 * Cos i / Square Root 30 * Sin i pow 2 + 45 * Cos i pow 2]

Figure-84. Formula for x position

- Right-click on the boundary of main block and select **Duplicate** option from the shortcut menu; refer to Figure-85. A copy of the block will be created.

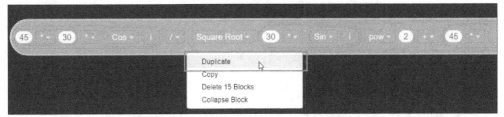

Figure-85. Duplicating block

- In this duplicate copy, change **Cos** option to **Sin** in first Math function block at the left; refer to Figure-86. This block will represent Y position on the ellipse.

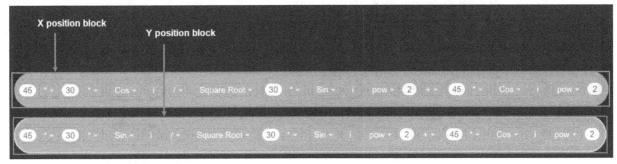

Figure-86. X and Y blocks for positioning

- Drag these blocks and put them in **X** and **Y** input boxes of the **Move** block earlier placed; refer to Figure-87.

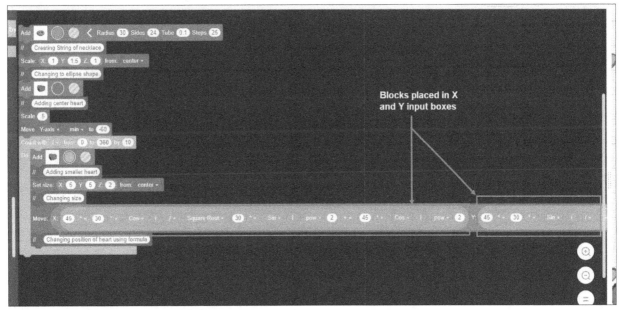

Figure-87. Placing blocks in Move block

- Place **Create Group** block below the **Count-Do** block to combine components of necklace to a single object for sharing with others.
- On running the codes, a necklace will be generated in the 3D Viewer; refer to Figure-88.

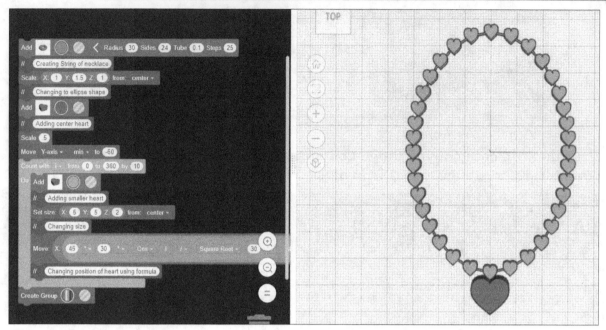

Figure-88. Final model

Chapter 3

Circuits

Topics Covered

The major topics covered in this chapter are:

- *Starting Circuit Design*
- *Basic Components*
- *All Components*
- *Basic Starters*
- *Schematic View*
- *Components List*

INTRODUCTION TO CIRCUIT DESIGN

Circuit design is the process of arranging wires and electrical/electronic components such that they can perform a specific function. It involves selecting and arranging electronic components, such as resistors, capacitors, transistors, and integrated circuits (ICs), in a way that enables them to work together to achieve the desired outcome. Circuit design can be as simple as creating a basic light switch circuit or as complex as designing the microprocessor inside a computer.

STARTING CIRCUIT DESIGN

- Click on the **+Create** button from the application window, the three options will be displayed; refer to Figure-1. Click on the **Circuits** button, the user interface of **Circuits** workspace will be displayed; refer to Figure-2. Various elements of this user interface are discussed next.

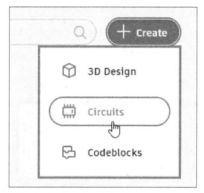

Figure-1. Create options

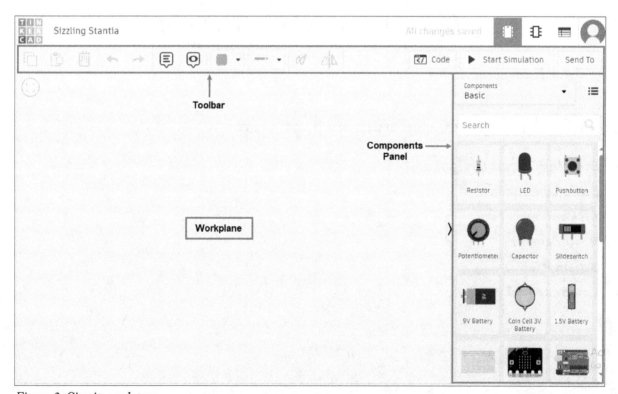

Figure-2. Circuits workspace

Toolbar

Most of the tools of the toolbar has been discussed earlier. Rest of the tools are discussed next.

Notes tool

The **Notes** tool is used to add desired note in the design. Generally, it is used to show comments or prompts about a component or circuit. The procedure to use this tool is discussed next.

• Click on the **Notes** tool from the toolbar; refer to Figure-3 and drag it to the workplane. A notes box will be placed; refer to Figure-4.

Figure-3. Notes tool

Figure-4. Notes box

• Write desired note in the box displayed.
• To delete the note, select the note and click on the **Del** button from the keyboard.

Toggle notes visibility

• Toggle the **Toggle notes visibility** tool from toolbar to ON or OFF the visibility of created notes; refer to Figure-5.

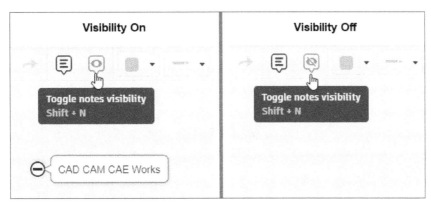

Figure-5. Toggle notes visibility tool

Wire color

The **Wire color** tool is used to change color of the wire to be drawn in graphics area. The procedure to use this tool is discussed next.

- Select desired wire from the workplane whose color is to be changed and click on the **Wire color** tool from the toolbar; refer to Figure-6. The **WIRE COLOR** drop-down will be displayed; refer to Figure-7.

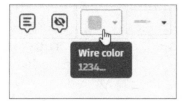

Figure-6. Wire color tool

Figure-7. WIRE COLOR drop down

- Select desired color from the drop-down. The color of selected wire and subsequent wires that you are going to create will be changed; refer to Figure-8.

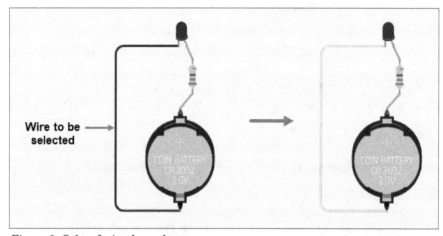

Figure-8. Color of wire changed

Wire type

The **Wire type** tool is used to change the type of the wire. The procedure to use this tool is discussed next.

- Select desired wire from the workplane whose type is to be changed and click on the **Wire type** tool from the toolbar; refer to Figure-9. The **WIRE TYPE** drop-down will be displayed; refer to Figure-10.

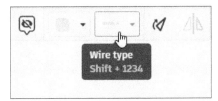

Figure-9. Wire type tool

Figure-10. WIRE TYPE drop down

- Click on desired type of wire from the drop-down. The type of wire will be changed; refer to Figure-11. You can also switch between different wire types of selected wire by pressing **SHIFT+1**, **SHIFT+2**, **SHIFT+3**, and **SHIFT+4** keys.

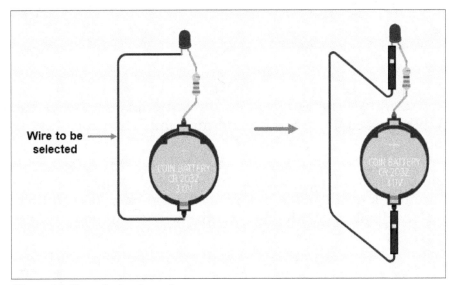

Figure-11. Type of wire changed

Rotate

The **Rotate** tool is used to rotate selected component in the workplane. The procedure to use this tool is discussed next.

- Select desired component from the workplane to be rotated and click on the **Rotate** tool from the toolbar. The component will be rotated; refer to Figure-12. Note that once you click on the tool, the component will rotate by **30°**.

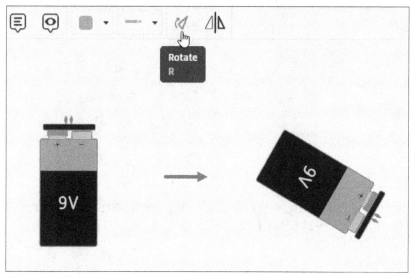

Figure-12. Component rotated

Code

The **Code** tool is used to write program codes using text or blocks coding language for programmable devices like Arduino and microbit. The procedure to use this tool is discussed next.

• Create desired assembly of multiple circuits with programmable devices to be simulated and click on the **Code** tool from the toolbar; refer to Figure-13. A code editor box will be displayed with related codes written in the box for the simulation; refer to Figure-14.

Figure-13. Code tool

Figure-14. Code editor box

- Click on the **Change the edit mode** button and select desired edit mode of the code from the drop-down list.
- Click on the **Download code** button to download the code in **INO** format to be used with Arduino software.
- Click on the **Libraries** button to get the library of codes to be used with Arduino software.
- Click on the **Font size** button and select desired font for the code.
- Click on the **Select device** button and select desired device to run the code for simulation.
- After specifying desired parameters in the code editor box, click on the **Start Simulation** button from the toolbar; refer to Figure-15. The simulation will be started.

Figure-15. Start Simulation tool

Blocks mode

You can modify the programming codes of the circuit using blocks in the **Blocks** mode of code editor; refer to Figure-16.

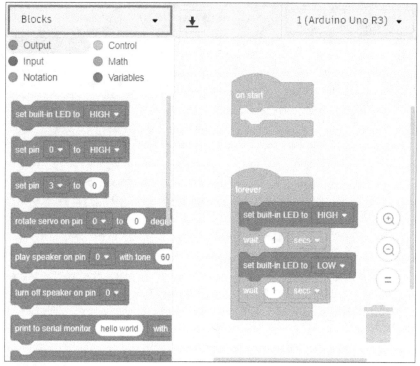

Figure-16. Blocks mode of coding

Blocks + Text mode

You can modify the programming codes of the circuit using blocks as well as using text in the **Blocks + Text** mode of code editor; refer to Figure-17.

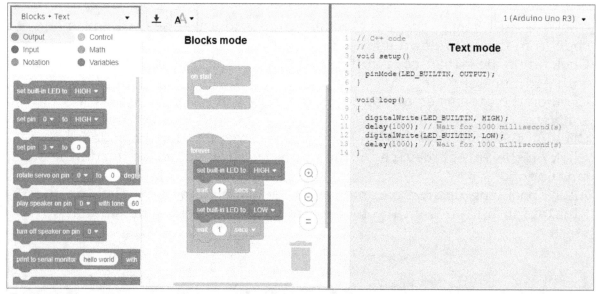

Figure-17. Blocks + Text mode of code

Text mode

You can modify the programming code of the circuit using only text in the **Text** mode of code editor; refer to Figure-18. Note that C++ programming language is used for Arduino and ATTINY whereas Python language is used for Microbit and Microbit with breakout devices.

```
Text                    ▼   ↓  ▣  A̅A̲ ▼   1 (Arduino Uno R3) ▼

1  // C++ code
2  //
3  void setup()
4  {
5    pinMode(LED_BUILTIN, OUTPUT);
6  }
7
8  void loop()
9  {
10   digitalWrite(LED_BUILTIN, HIGH);
11   delay(1000); // Wait for 1000 millisecond(s)
12   digitalWrite(LED_BUILTIN, LOW);
13   delay(1000); // Wait for 1000 millisecond(s)
14 }
```

Figure-18. Text mode of coding

BASIC COMPONENT

Select the **Basic** option from the **Components Library** drop-down. The tools to place basic components will be displayed as shown in Figure-19. Various commonly used components of this library are discussed next.

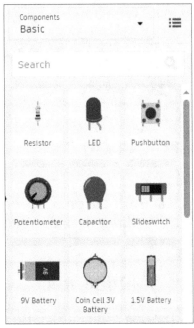

Figure-19. Basic component tools

Resistor

The **Resistor** tool is used to place resistor in the workplane which restricts the flow of electricity in a circuit hence reducing the voltage and current. The procedure to use this tool is discussed next.

- Click on the **Resistor** tool from the **Basic Components** library and drag it to the workplane. The resistor will be placed in the workplane and the **Resistor** dialog box will be displayed; refer to Figure-20.

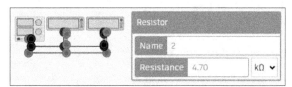

Figure-20. Resistor dialog box

- Specify desired name and resistance of the resistor in the **Name** and **Resistance** edit boxes, respectively.
- Select desired unit of the resistance from drop-down in the dialog box.
- After specifying desired parameters, click in the workplane to exit the dialog box.

LED

The LED (Light-Emitting Diode) is an object that lights up when electricity passes through it in the correct direction. The procedure to use this tool is discussed next.

- Click on the **LED** tool from the **Basic Components** library and drag it to the workplane. The led will be placed in the workplane and the **LED** dialog box will be displayed; refer to Figure-21.

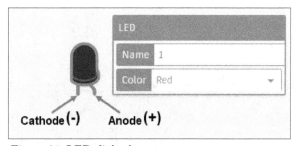

Figure-21. LED dialog box

- Select desired color of the LED from **Color** drop-down in the dialog box.
- Specify other parameters in the dialog box as discussed earlier and click in the workplane to exit the dialog box.

Multimeter

The **Multimeter** tool is used for measuring voltage, current, and resistance in your circuit. The procedure to use this tool is discussed next.

- Click on the **Multimeter** tool from the **Basic Components** library and drag it to the workplane. The multimeter will be placed in the workplane and the **Multimeter** dialog box will be displayed; refer to Figure-22.

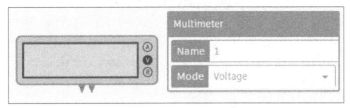

Figure-22. Multimeter dialog box

- Select desired mode of measurement from the **Mode** drop-down in the dialog box. For example, if you want to measure voltage then select the **Voltage** option from the **Mode** drop-down.
- Specify other parameters in the dialog box as discussed earlier and click in the workplane to exit the dialog box.

Similarly, you can place other basic components. Brief descriptions about major components in **Basic** library are given next.

Push button

Push button is a switch that closes a circuit on pressing the switch. Refer to Figure-23.

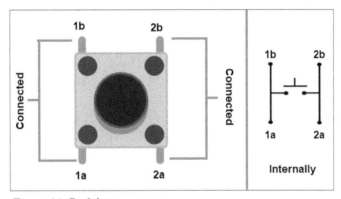

Figure-23. Push button

Capacitor

Capacitor is used to store and release electrical energy in a circuit. Refer to Figure-24. It can work as filter to provide constant supply of current or stop DC signals while allowing AC signals. It can act as time delaying tool in electronic circuit. There are many other uses of capacitors in electrical and electronic circuits. The value of capacitor is measured in picoFarad (pF) to GigaFarad(GF). A non-polarized capacitor has no polarity bias, so pin-wise they can be connected either-way.

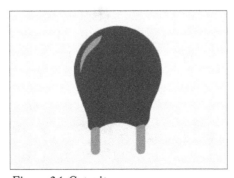

Figure-24. Capacitor

Potentiometer

Potentiometer is also called pot and pot meter in slang language by electronic enthusiasts. It is a variable resistor with three terminals. It is generally used to control voltage at the center terminal also called Wiper; refer to Figure-25. The potentiometer is polarity neutral so you can connect it either way in circuit. The potentiometers are rated by their resistance in ohm (Ω).

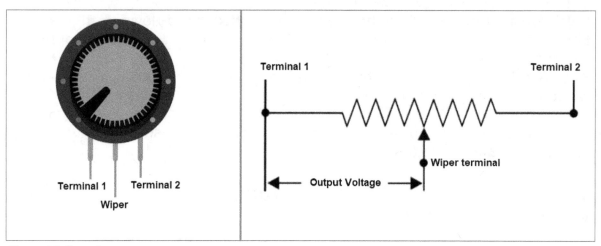

Figure-25. Potentiometer

Slide switch

Slide switch is a switch with open and closed positions. Refer to Figure-26. You can supply current to only one terminal of the two when supply is connected to common. This switch can also be used in reverse. For example, you have two source of power supply connected at Terminal 1 and Terminal 2 of the switch they you can use the switch to choose between two supplies for providing current at common point.

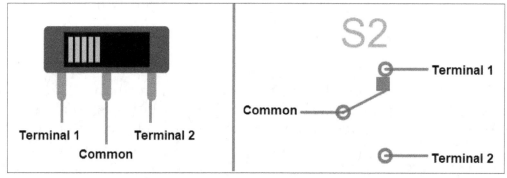

Figure-26. Slideswitch

9V Battery

9V Battery is a common battery that is great for higher power applications like motors. Refer to Figure-27.

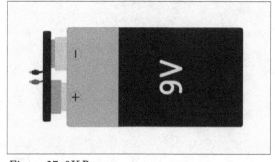

Figure-27. 9V Battery

Coin Cell 3V Battery

Coin Cell 3V Battery is a small battery great for low power applications like lighting up LEDs. Refer to Figure-28.

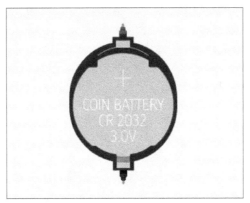

Figure-28. Coin Cell 3V Battery

1.5V Battery

The 1.5V Battery is a standard AA or AAA batteries, with each battery providing 1.5V. The procedure to use this tool is discussed next.

- Click on the **1.5V Battery** tool from the **Basic Components** library and drag it to the workplane. The 1.5V battery will be placed in the workplane and the **1.5V Battery** dialog box will be displayed; refer to Figure-29.

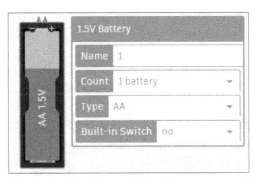

Figure-29. 1.5V battery dialog box

- Select desired number and type of battery in the **Count** and **Type** drop-down, respectively.
- Select desired option from **Built in Switch** drop-down if you want to display an ON/OFF switch on the battery or not.
- Specify other parameters in the dialog box as discussed earlier and click in the workplane to exit the dialog box.

Breadboard Small

Breadboard Small is a half-size breadboard with 30 rows, 10 columns, and two pairs of power rails. Refer to Figure-30. If you are not familiar with breadboard then it is a board used by electronic circuit designers and enthusiasts to connect various electronic components without soldering and perform tests on it. In a breadboard, all the points in same rows (marked by 1, 2, 3...) are connected together. Similarly, all points in **+** column are connected together and all points in **-** column are connected together; refer to Figure-31.

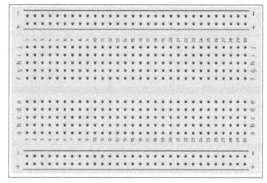

Figure-30. Breadboard Small

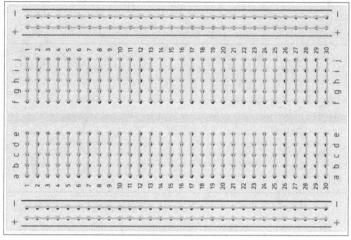

Figure-31. Connections in breadboard

micro:bit and Arduino Uno R3

The micro:bit and Arduino Uno R3 are programmable boards used to build interactive circuits; refer to Figure-32. A Micro:bit has in built sensors like temperature sensor, light sensor, accelerometer, and compass. Arduino does not have any in-built sensor but there are many input/output terminals that can be used to facilitate external sensors. Details about various pins of these devices are given next.

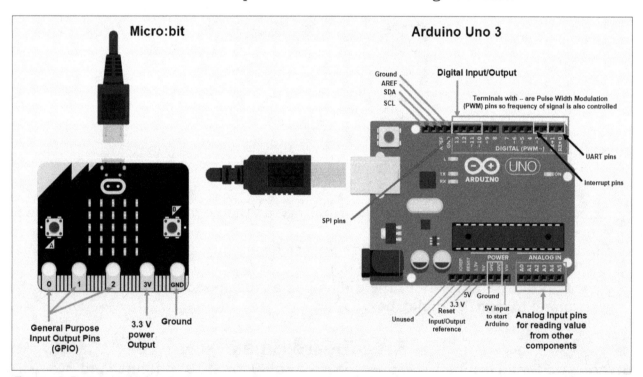

Figure-32. Programmable boards

Microbit Pins

- Pin 0, 1, and 2 of Microbit are General Purpose Input/Output pins with analog to digital convertor. In short, also called GPIO with ADC. You can read both digital and analog signals as well as output them using these pins.

- Pin 3V can be used as power output of 3.3 voltage or it can be used as power input to run Micro:bit if USB power is not being supplied.
- GND pin is used to connect to ground of power supply for completing the circuit.

Arduino Uno Pins

- The pins SCL, SDA, AREF, and Ground on top left side of Arduino board are used to setup communication line for I2C protocol. The components that support I2C protocol will use these pins for connection. Use SCL pin to connect clock line, use SDA pin to connect data line, use AREF pin to connect to voltage that will be used as reference for measurement; refer to QR code given next. Arduino comes with a 10bit ADC (Analog-Digital-Converter), which converts incoming voltages between 0V and 5V to integer values between 0 and 1023 by default. If your sensor has voltage range of 3V for functioning and you want to have accurate measurement of the voltage at which your component is running then you should connect 3V supply to the AREF pin and then use Analog pins to perform measurement. Use the Ground pin to ground all the circuits. Note that when you are using I2C protocol, it is important to select same address for component on the I2C bus to which you want to send the signals. You can connect multiple components to same wires and configure them at different addresses to work with them; refer to Figure-33. Note that in Arduino, pin A4 and A5 can also be used as Data and Clock lines, respectively.

Using
AREF Pin

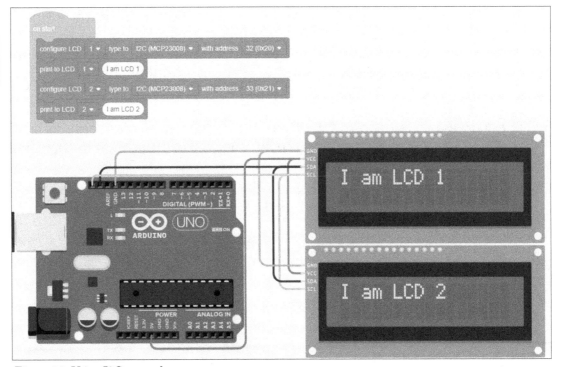

Figure-33. Using I2C protocol

- The digital I/O pins 13, 12, 11, and 10 can be used for SPI protocol to control multiple components and devices that support SPI protocol. The connection speed in SPI protocol is faster than I2C and UART protocols. Pin 13 represents SCK pin (clock), pin 12 represents MISO pin (Master In, Slave out), pin 11 represents MOSI (Master Out, Slave In), and pin 10 represents SS (Slave Select). Using MOSI pin, master device like Arduino sends signal to external device and using MISO pin, Arduino received signal from the external device. SCK pin is used to define at what clock speed the signals are being sent. SS pin defines to which device the master device is talking. Multiple slave devices are connected and differentiated by SS pins; refer to Figure-34.

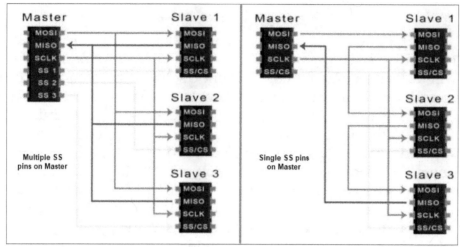

Figure-34. SPI protocol

- The digital input/output pin 0 (RX) and pin 1 (TX) can be used for receiving and sending signals using UART protocol to connected components that support UART serial communication. You can also connect 2 or more Arduino by using these pins.
- Pin 0 to 13 in Digital section can be used as digital input and output pins which means you can send and receive signals by using these pins. Pin 3, 5, 6, 9, 10, and 11 can be used to send and receive Pulse width modulated signals.
- Pin A0 to A5 can be used to send and receive analog signals.
- Use the Vin pin to supply power to the Arduino if you do not want to use USB power supply.
- The IOREF pin is used to tell other connected micro controllers about the voltage at which this device is working so that they can adjust their voltage when sending/ receiving signals.
- The Reset pin is used to reset the operation of Arduino and everything starts from beginning. You need to ground this reset pin with a push button to control it.

Vibration Motor

A Vibration Motor is a motor that vibrates when plugged in. Refer to Figure-35.

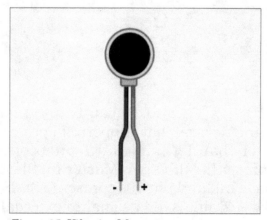

Figure-35. Vibration Motor

DC Motor

DC Motor is used to convert electrical energy into mechanical energy. Refer to Figure-36.

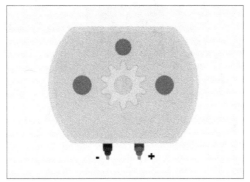

Figure-36. DC Motor

Micro Servo

Micro Servo is a motor whose position can be controlled using a micro controller like Arduino; refer to Figure-37.

Hobby Gearmotor

Hobby Gearmotor is a geared motor that is used to drive robot wheels; refer to Figure-38. Generally, RPM of motor is reduced by using gears so that it does not rotate at very high RPM. Connecting power source in reverse polarity will make the motor rotate in reverse direction.

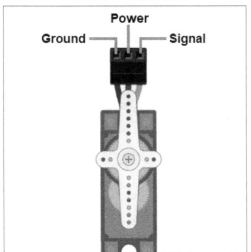

Figure-37. Micro Servo

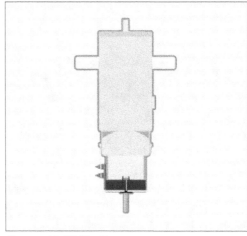

Figure-38. Hobby Gearmotor

NPN Transistor (BJT)

NPN Transistor (Bipolar Junction Transistor) is used to amplify or switch electronic signals. It is commonly used with motors. The transistor has three terminals: Collector (C), Base (B), and Emitter (E); refer to Figure-39 and Figure-40. When using transistor as amplifier- weak signal is provided at Base terminal and strong signal is received at Collector terminal. Note that the current supplied at Emitter terminal is added to signal at Base terminal to produce amplified signal. When using NPN transistor as switch, the current flows from collector to emitter only if sufficient voltage is applied to Base terminal otherwise the connection remains OFF. Due to this ON/OFF property, transistors are also used in digital circuits as gates.

Figure-39. NPN Transistor

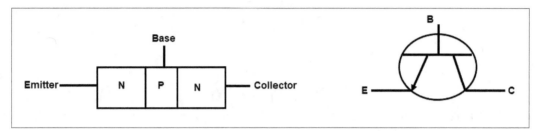

Figure-40. NPN Transistor

LED RGB

LED RGB is a type of LED that combines Red, Blue, and Green colors to produce any color. Refer to Figure-41.

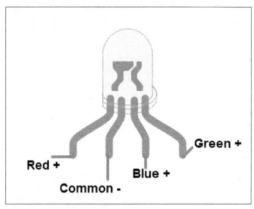

Figure-41. LED RGB

Diode

Diode allows electricity to flow in only one direction; refer to Figure-42. The current flows from anode (+) to cathode (-); refer to Figure-43.

Figure-42. Diode

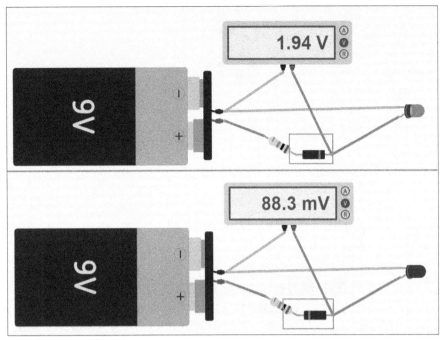

Figure-43. Use of diode

Photoresistor

Photoresistor is a sensor whose resistance changes based on the amount of light it senses. Refer to Figure-44. After placing photoresistor in circuit, you can control amount of light during simulation by using slider displayed on selecting the photo resistor; refer to Figure-45.

Figure-44. Photoresistor

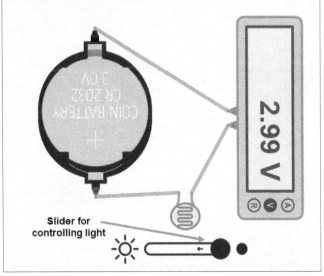

Figure-45. Using Photoresistor

Soil Moisture Sensor

Soil Moisture Sensor is a sensor whose signal voltage changes on getting wet. Refer to Figure-46. This sensor is generally used to detect moisture in agricultural land hence, managing irrigation requirement of land. It can also be used to measure rainfall and forecast climate.

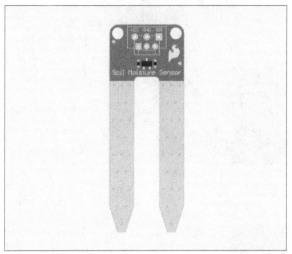

Figure-46. Soil Moisture Sensor

Ultrasonic Distance Sensor

Ultrasonic Distance Sensor is a sensor that uses sound waves to determine the distance of an object. Refer to Figure-47. Connect power to GND and 5V terminals of the sensor to supply voltage and you will receive signal in the form of distance to object at the SIG terminal. Generally, this SIG terminal is connected to programmable device like Arduino to perform different operations; refer to Figure-48.

Figure-47. Ultrasonic Distance Sensor

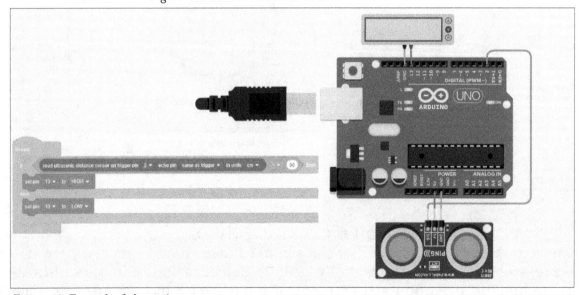

Figure-48. Example of ultrasonic sensor

PIR Sensor

PIR Sensor is a passive infrared motion sensor used to sense motion in front of the sensor; refer to Figure-49. The functioning of this sensor is similar to Ultrasonic distance sensor as far as circuit designing is concerned. At functional level, this sensor uses infrared waves to detect movement of objects rather than measuring distance. Example circuit is shown in Figure-50.

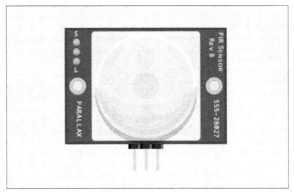

Figure-49. PIR Sensor

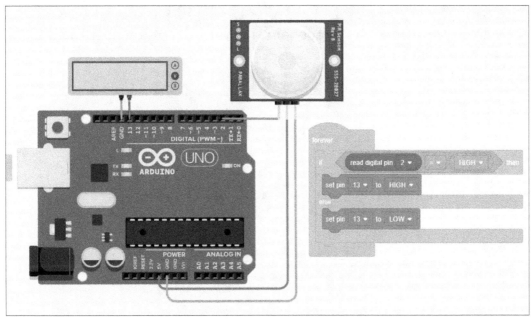

Figure-50. PIR sensor circuit example

Piezo

Piezo is a type of buzzer that makes noise at different frequencies; refer to Figure-51. This buzzer is generally used to sound alarms or notifications when performing circuit operation.

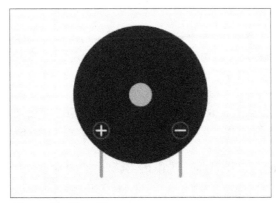

Figure-51. Piezo Buzzer

Temperature Sensor (TMP36)

Temperature Sensor is a sensor that outputs different voltages based on the ambient temperature; refer to Figure-52.

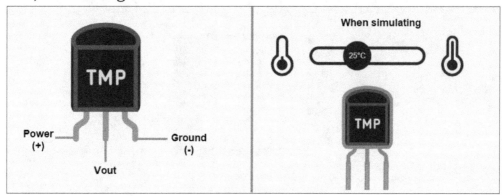

Figure-52. Temperature Sensor

ALL COMPONENT

Select the **All** button from the **Components** library drop-down. All the tools will be displayed; refer to Figure-53.

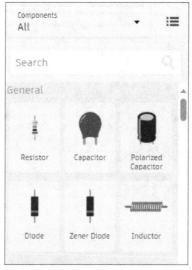

Figure-53. All component tools

Polarized Capacitor

The **Polarized Capacitor** is a directional capacitor used to store and release electric energy in a circuit. It allows current to pass in one direction. The procedure to use this tool is discussed next.

- Click on the **Polarized Capacitor** tool from the **General** section in the **All Components** library and drag it to the workplane. The polarized capacitor will be placed and the **Polarized Capacitor** dialog box will be displayed; refer to Figure-54.
- Specify desired capacitance and voltage rating in the **Capacitance** and **Voltage Rating** edit boxes, respectively and select desired units from the respective drop-downs.
- Specify other parameters in the dialog box as discussed earlier and click in the workplane to exit the dialog box.

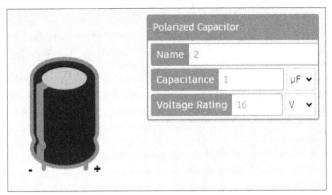

Figure-54. Polarized Capacitor dialog box

Zener Diode

The Zener diode works in opposite direction to Diode which has been discussed earlier. It allows current to flow in reverse direction when certain voltage threshold is crossed across the terminals.

Inductor

The Inductor is used to store electrical energy in the form of magnetic field and supply it back instantaneously when power source is removed from the circuit.

Photodiode

A Photodiode generates electricity in the presence of light (photons). Photodiodes are used in solar cells, fire and smoke safety devices, medical instruments, calculators, and so on.

Ambient Light Sensor

The Ambient Light Sensor is used to generate a small voltage signal (3.33 milliVolt) in the presence of light. This signal can be used to control other operation using Arduino or other programmable boards. Connect **C** terminal to positive and **E** terminal to negative/ground in circuit.

Flex Sensor

As the name suggests, flex sensor changes its resistance value based on how much flexed (bent) it is. The more you bend it, the more will be its resistance value.

Force Sensor

The Force sensor changes its resistance value based on forces applied at its face. Generally, load detection is performed by this sensor like in your car seats to display seat belt reminders.

IR Sensor

The IR sensor is used to detect infrared radiation emitting from hot objects or infrared signal sent by IR remotes. In most of the televisions, you will find IR sensors paired with IR remotes.

Ultrasonic Distance Sensor (HC-SR04)

The Ultrasonic Distance Sensor (HC-SR04) does the same work what ultra sonic distance sensor does which has been discussed earlier. But this sensor has a different pinout; refer to Figure-55. Vcc pin is connected to power supply, GND is connected to Ground, TRIG pin is connected to an output pin on Arduino, and ECHO is connected to input pin on Arduino. At TRIG pin, we provide signal to define duration for which sonar on ultrasonic sensor will send waves. This value is specified in microseconds. At the ECHO pin, high signal is generated when receiving back the sonar waves reflected by object; refer to Figure-56.

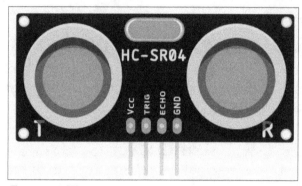

Figure-55. Ultrasonic Distance Sensor SR04

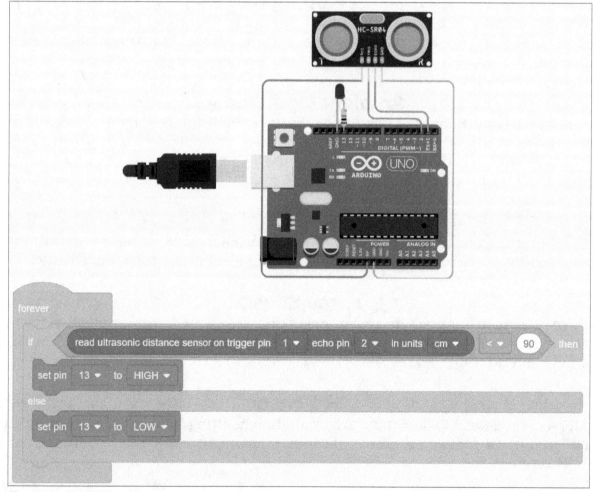

Figure-56. Using Ultrasonic sensor

Tilt Sensor

The Tilt sensor is used to detect tilting of object with respect to defined axis. This sensor works as a variable resistor with a small conductive ball or liquid conductive solution used as connection point on metal strip. There are many types of tilt sensors which can give readings of tilt apart from connecting/disconnecting circuit at certain angle threshold. In Tinkercad, you will get a tilt sensor which connects the circuit after certain tilt of sensor and disconnects the circuit if sensor is not tilted; refer to Figure-57.

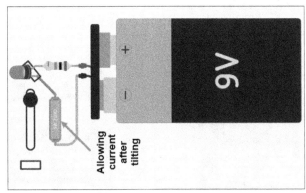

Figure-57. Using Tilt sensor

Gas Sensor

The Gas sensor used in Tinkercad is Semiconductor / Metal Oxide-based Gas Sensor which has six terminals. The mid two terminals H1 and H2 are used to supply current for heating inner elements (a coil of Nickel-chromium) which in turn burns the sensing element of gas sensing layer (generally Tin Oxide). Based on gas entering in the sensor, resistance of gas sensing layer changes and hence changing the resistance between A and B terminals. Note that A1 and A2 are connected internally and similarly, B1 and B2 are connected internally. Figure-58 shows the basic functioning of gas sensor.

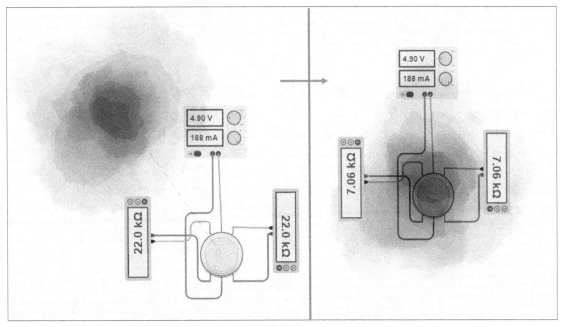

Figure-58. Gas sensor working

Keypad 4x4

The Keypad is used to input numbers and characters in programmable devices like Arduino. In any keypad input device, terminals are created depending on number of columns and rows. Since, our 4x4 keypad has 4 columns and 4 rows so there are 4 terminals for columns and 4 terminals for rows. If you want to know what happens when you press a key then you need to simulate the circuit as shown in Figure-59. On pressing a key, the terminals for row and column of the pressed key gets shorted means resistance between these terminals becomes zero. This can be achieved mechanically or by digital gate circuits as well. When using Keypad as input device, you can connect terminals of the keypad to digital pins of Arduino.

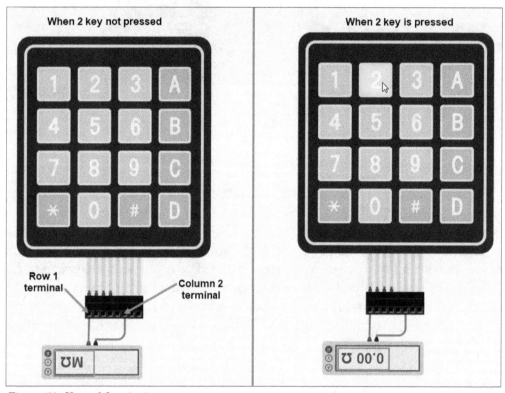

Figure-59. Keypad functioning

DIP Switch DPST

The DIP stands for Dual Inline Packaging is used when you want to package multiple switches or integrated circuits in a plastic packaging. In this packaging, all the terminals of component are arranged in two rows with legs coming out of plastic packaging. DPST stands for Double Pole Single Through which represents two switches connected together and controlled by single button; refer to Figure-60 on how terminals get connected on switching the DPST switch ON.

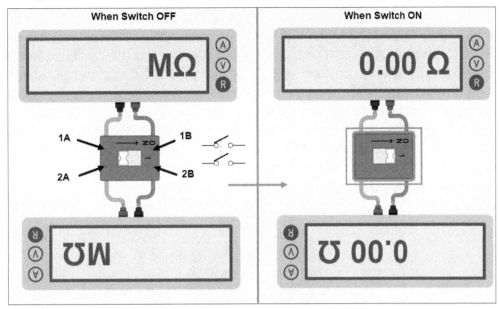

Figure-60. DIP Switch DPST

DIP Switch SPST x 4 and DIP Switch SPST x 6

SPST stands for Single Pole Single Through which means single switch is controlled by pushing the related button and no other switch will be altered by that button. The placement and connection procedures of DIP Switch SPSTx4 and DIP Switch SPSTx6 are similar to DIP Switch DPST.

Light Bulb

The light bulb is available in the **Output** section of **Components** panel. It is used in same applications where LED is employed. There are two main differences in using light bulb against LED: Light bulb is polarity neutral which means you can interchange live and ground wire without affecting operation of bulb. The heat generated by Light bulb is much greater than LED, so applications of light bulb are suitable in lighting rooms and spaces.

NeoPixel

The NeoPixel is a small board or strip with multiple LEDs embedded on it. These LEDs can change color and they can be controlled individually by using signals provided through programmable devices. The functions of various pins on NeoPixel LEDs are shown in Figure-61. To control colors of LEDs in this component, we use functions of Adafruit NeoPixel library of Arduino.

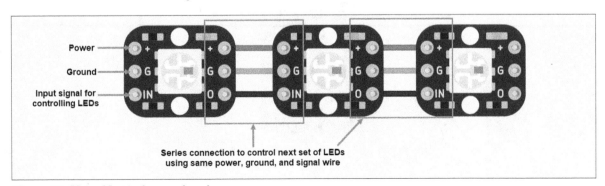

Figure-61. Using Neopixel square board

Similarly, you can use NeoPixel Rings and Strips of different sizes to your circuit.

DC Motor with Encoder

The DC motor with encoder is a motor that also provides precise control over speed, position, and direction of motor. A small PCB with encoder circuit is attached the motor to provide signals for motor speed, position, and direction. The pin detail of this motor in Tinkercad is shown in Figure-62. Connect + terminal of power source with positive terminal of Motor and Power terminal of Encoder. Similarly, you can connect ground terminals of motor and encoder with - terminal of power source or Arduino. Connect Channel A and Channel B terminals to Digital input pins of Arduino to get data signals from encoder of motor. Note that you will need a Motor Driver IC to control speed of motor based on encoder signals.

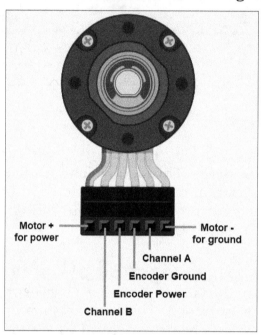

Figure-62. Motor with encoder

IR Remote

IR Remote is used to broadcast infrared signals on pressing its buttons; refer to Figure-63. You will need IR sensor to receive the signal sent by IR remote to perform actions.

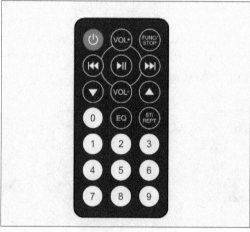

Figure-63. IR remote

7 Segment Display

The 7 Segment Display is used to show single digit from 0-9 based on provided signal. The pin details of display are shown in Figure-64. When power is supplied to terminal A then A segment of display will light up. Similarly, other terminals are related to respective segments of display. On placing this display in working area, the option to set common terminal as Cathode or Anode will be displayed; refer to Figure-65. Generally, common terminal is set to Cathode (-) so that power can be supplied to other pins using digital pins on Arduino. You can reverse it by selecting **Anode** option from the drop-down if your project demands.

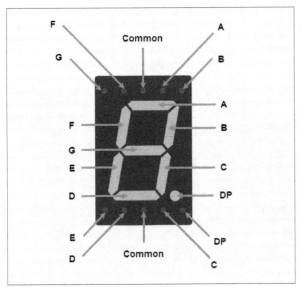

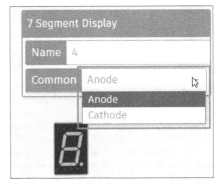

Figure-65. Option for 7Segment Display

Figure-64. Terminal and related led on 7-segment display

LCD 16 x 2

The LCD 16 x 2 is used to display information generated by programming Arduino and other programmable devices. The Pin details of the LCD are shown in Figure-66.

- Connect power source positive to Power pin (VCC) and power source negative to Ground pin.
- Connect a power source regulated by potentiometer to the V0 pin for adjusting contrast of LCD screen.
- Connect Register Selection pin (RS) to a digital data output pin of Arduino. When you send 0 to this pin then LCD will use command register and when you send 1 to this pin then LCD will use data register. Using Command register, you can send commands like clear screen, change color, change size, and so on. When Data register is selected then you can send data to be displayed on LCD screen.
- Connect Read/Write Mode pin to digital data output pin of Arduino. When 0 is sent to this pin then writing mode is active which means you can write data using the DB pins on LCD screen. This can be performed by grounding this pin apart from digitally sending 0. When 1 is sent to this pin (set to High), then LCD will work in read mode. You can use same DB pins to read from LCD using LiquidCrystal library of C programming.
- Connect the Enable pin to digital output pin on Arduino. When 1 is sent to this pin, the LCD will be active and display as per commands. When 0 is sent to this pin, the LCD will be inactive and it will ignore the commands sent to it. You can consider it as digital ON/OFF switch for LCD.

- The DB0 to DB7 pins represent 8 bits that can be sent to display at one time. The LCD can work in 4 bit mode and 8 bit mode. Connect only DB4 to DB7 if you want to work in 4 bit mode and connect all 8 pins to work in 8 bits mode. In 4 bit mode, less pins are required on Arduino but processing time is high due to more cycles for sending the same data. Reverse is true for 8 bit mode.
- Connect LED Anode and LED Cathode to positive and negative terminals of power source with a resistor in series to provide power to backlight.

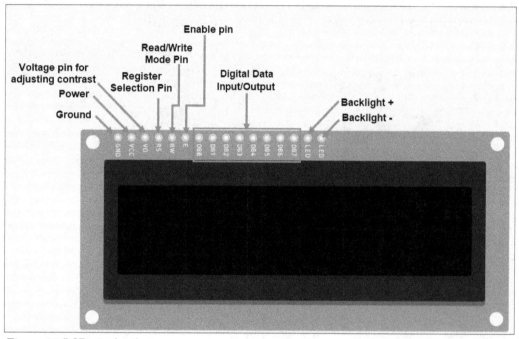

Figure-66. LCD pin details

LCD 16 x 2 (I2C)

The LCD 16 x 2 (I2C) is used to display output generated by programmable devices like Arduino. I2C means Inter-integrated circuit which means multiple ICs are inter connected to give you two pins SDA and SCL to perform same task as done by previous LCD with multiple pins. The pin details of this LCD are shown in Figure-67.

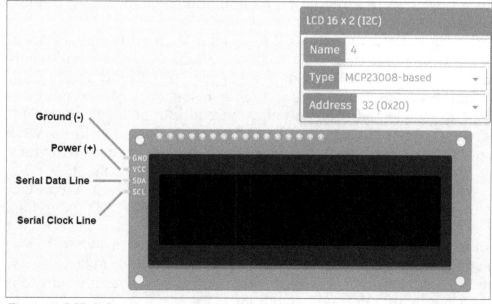

Figure-67. LCD I2C pins

- When placing the LCD in working area, you can set the type and address of LCD in respective fields of the LCD 16 x 2 (I2C) input box as shown in Figure-67. Select **PCF8574-based** option from **Type** drop-down if you want to use LiquidCrystal I2C library and select the MCP23008-based if you want to use Adafruit MCP23008 or Adafruit MCP23017 library.
- Set desired option in **Address** drop-down to define address on serial port where arduino will send commands to control LCD.
- Connect the Ground and VCC pins to Ground and Power terminals of power source. Note that voltage require is approximately 5V.
- Connect the Serial Data Line (SDA) pin with SDA pin of Arduino and Serial Clock Line pin to SCL pin of arduino as shown in Figure-68. You can use code blocks for programming these LCDs.

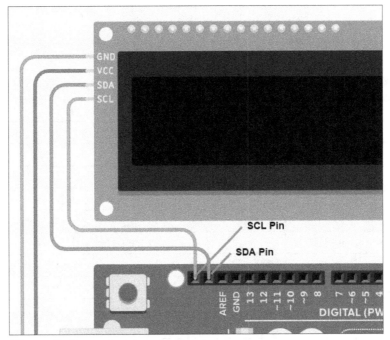

Figure-68. Connecting pins with Arduino

The procedures to use power sources like 9V battery, 1.5V Battery, etc. and Breadboards like small breadboard has been discussed earlier.

Micro:bit with Breakout

The procedure to use Micro:bit component has been discussed earlier. Micro:bit with breakout is a micro:bit device which gives more pins to work with allowing you to connect additional components like sensors, switches, motors, and so on; refer to Figure-69. The pin details of Micro:bit with Breakout are given next.

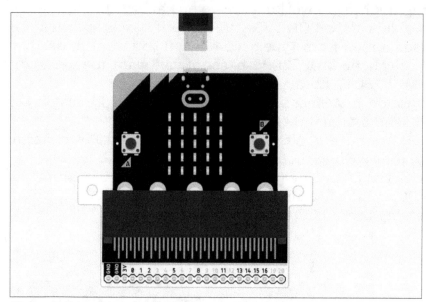

Figure-69. Micro bit with breakout pins

Pin	Function 1	Function 2	Description
GND			Ground
GND			Ground
3V3			3.3V
0	Analog In		Connected to large pin 0
1	Analog In		Connected to large pin 1
2	Analog In		Connected to large pin 2
3	Analog In	LED Column 1	Controls part of LED array
4	Analog In	LED Column 2	Controls part of LED array
5		Button A	Connected to Button A on micro:bit
6		LED Column 9	Controls part of LED array
7		LED Column 8	Controls part of LED array
8			Open GPIO pin
9		LED Column 7	Controls part of LED array
10	Analog In	LED Column 3	Controls part of LED array
11		Button B	Connected to Button B on micro:bit
12			Open GPIO pin
13	SCK		GPIO or SPI clock
14	MISO		GPIO or SPI MISO
15	MOSI		GPIO or SPI MOSI
16			Open GPIO pin
19	SCL		GPIO or I2 clock
20	SDA		GPIO or I2 data

ATTINY

ATTINY is a small microcontroller component that can be programmed to perform various operations; refer to Figure-70. There are 4 versions of Attiny chip available in market. The ATtiny84, ATtiny85, and the ATtiny2313, along with the ATmega328P, have a different number of I/O pins, different amounts of flash memory for program storage, and different numbers of ADC inputs and PWM outputs. Visit this QR code for pin details.

ATTINY pin details

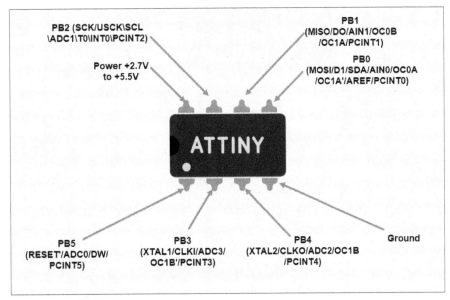

Figure-70. ATTINY pin details

In simple words, Pin PB0 to PB5 can be used as digital Input/Output pins and are mapped in sequence for block coding. So PB0 is digital pin 1, PB1 is digital pin 2, and so on. PB2 to PB5 are four analog to digital converted input pins. PB0 and PB1 can be used to output analog signals.

Function Generator

The Function Generator is used to generate Sine, Triangular, and Square electric signals using specified frequency, amplitude (max to min position on graph), DC Offset (amount of change either direction, positive to specify upper offset and negative to specify lower offset in wave graph), and function type. Figure-71 shows the use and display of created function in Serial Monitor.

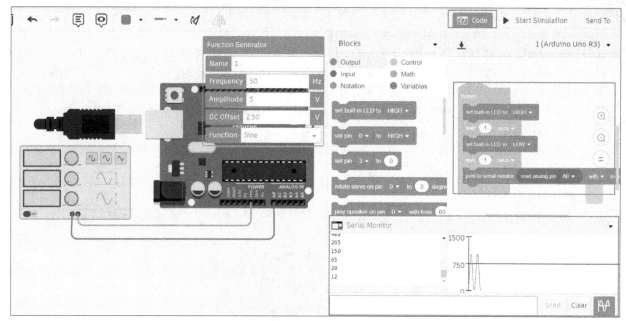

Figure-71. Using Function generator and Serial Monitor

Similarly, you can use Oscilloscope to check waveform of signal by connecting it to related pins.

Integrated Circuits

There are various IC (Integrated Circuits) chips available in the Integrated Circuits section of Components library to perform different operations in circuit. For example, 555 IC is used to program timer, delay, or pulse generator. Check data sheets and example circuits of these ICs to learn about their functions on internet.

Similarly, you can place other components of Power Control, Connectors, and Logic section of the Components library.

BASIC STARTERS

Starters are pre-built circuit examples designed to help you learn the basics of electronics and circuit building. The procedure to place these circuits of **Starters** library is same as discussed for components.

Schematic View

Click on the **Schematic View** from the toolbar; refer to Figure-72. The schematic drawing view of the circuit will be generated; refer to Figure-73. Click on the **Download .PDF** button at top right corner in schematic drawing view to generate and download PDF of the circuit being displayed.

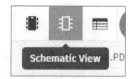

Figure-72. Schematic view tool

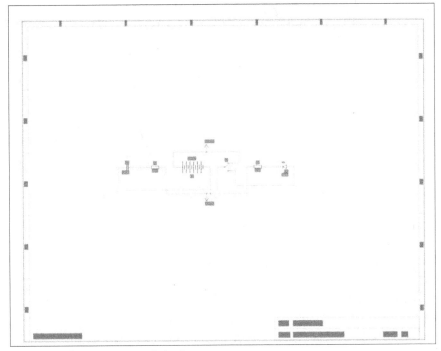

Figure-73. Schematic view dialog box

Component List

Click on the **Component List** tool from the toolbar to check list of all the components used in the circuit; refer to Figure-74. The list of the components in the circuit will be displayed; refer to Figure-75. Click on the **Download CSV** button from the top right corner in the working area to download list of components in CSV format.

Figure-74. Component list tool

Name	Quantity	Component
BAT7	1	9V Battery
S1	1	Slideswitch
R1 R2	2	100 Ω Resistor
C1	1	100 uF Capacitor
D1	1	Red LED
Meter9	1	Resistance Multimeter

Figure-75. List of the components

PRACTICAL 1

Create the circuit as shown in Figure-76.

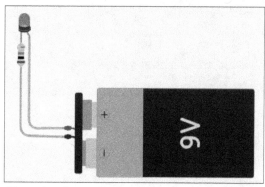

Figure-76. Circuit Practical 1

Steps

- Click on the **+Create** button from the **Tinkercad Application** window and select the **Circuit** option, the circuit workspace will be displayed.
- Click on the **Led** tool, **Resistor** tool, and **9V Battery** tool one by one & drag them to the workplane with placement as shown in Figure-77.

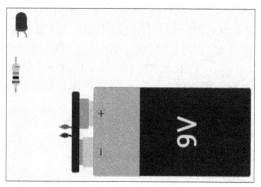

Figure-77. Dragging the circuit

- Drag the wire from **Anode** terminal of the led and place it to the **Positive** terminal of the 9V battery; refer to Figure-78.

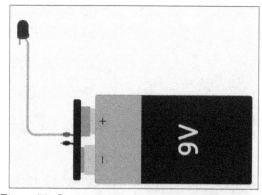

Figure-78. Connecting anode terminal with battery

- Click on the **Resistor** and drag the **Terminal 2** of resistor to the **Cathode** terminal of the led.
- Drag the wire from **Terminal 1** of the resistor and place it to the **Negative** terminal of the 9V battery; refer to Figure-79.

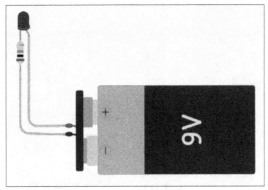

Figure-79. Resistor join negative terminal

- Now, click on the **Start Simulation** tool from the toolbar. The simlation of led will be started and the led will glow.
- If you want to measure the voltage to across any component then you can place the multimeter as shown in Figure-80.

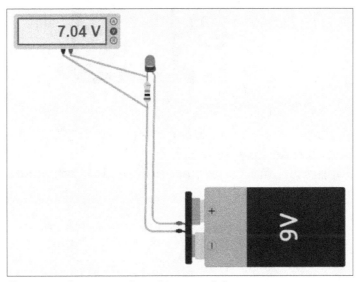

Figure-80. Connecting the multimeter to led

PRACTICAL 2

Create a circuit as shown in Figure-81 where motor starts to rotate when motion is detected by the PIR sensor. This circuit can be installed in mouse traps.

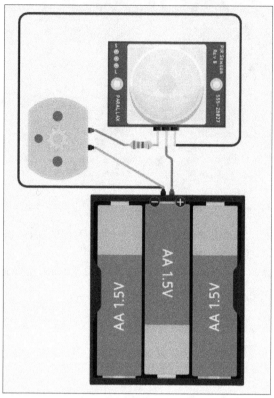

Figure-81. Circuit Practical 2

Steps

- Start a new circuit as discussed earlier.
- Select the **Basic** option from **Starter** section in the **Components** drop-down of the **Components** panel; refer to Figure-82.

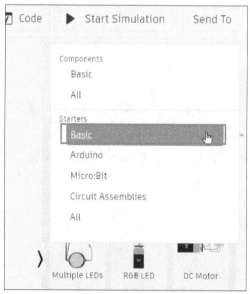

Figure-82. Basic Starters option

• Select the **PIR Sensor** starter circuit and place it in the workplane; refer to Figure-83.

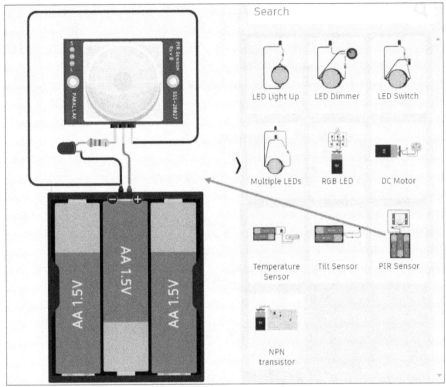

Figure-83. Placing PIR starter circuit

• Select the Red LED from the working area and press **DELETE** key from keyboard to delete it. The circuit will display as shown in Figure-84.

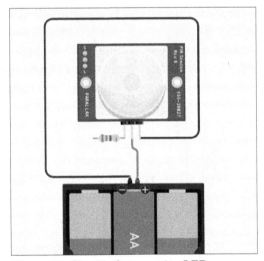

Figure-84. Circuit after removing LED

• Select **Basic** option from the drop-down at top in the **Components Library** and drag DC Motor in the circuit as shown in Figure-85. Rotate the motor and connect wires as shown in Figure-86. Note that we have changed the color of ground wire to green and power wire to red.

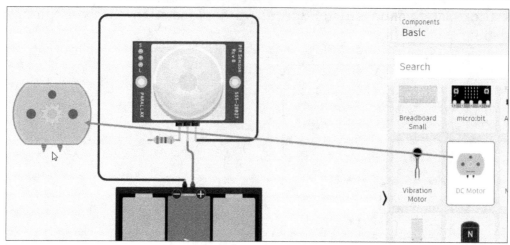

Figure-85. Placing motor

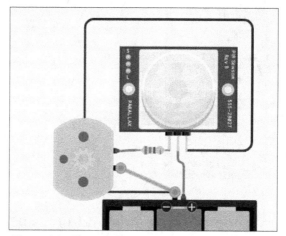

Figure-86. After connecting wires

- Drag the black wire and DC motor to non-overlapping positions to clean the circuit view; refer to Figure-87. Now, click on the **Start Simulation** tool from the toolbar. The simulation of DC motor will start. Note that motor will rotate only when motion sensor detects a motion; refer to Figure-88.

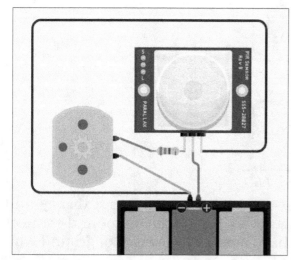

Figure-87. Cleaning circuit

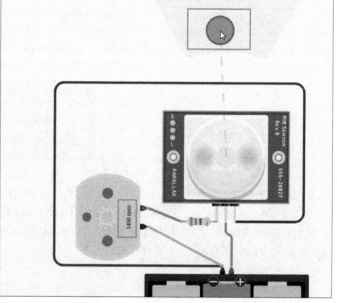

Figure-88. Simulating circuit

PRACTICAL 3

Create a circuit using four ultrasonic sensors that can detect distance of objects from car in all four directions and send alert on LCD when distance is below 45 centimeters as shown in Figure-89.

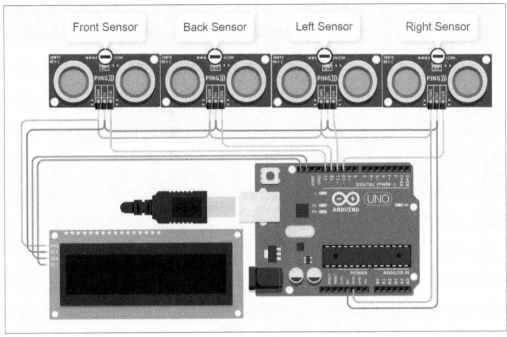

Figure-89. Circuit Practical 3

Steps

- Start a new circuit as discussed earlier.
- Click & drag 4 **Ultrasonic Distance Sensors**, 1 **Arduino Uno R3**, and 1 **LCD 16 x 2 (I2C)** in the working area and place them as shown in Figure-90. Make sure LCD is set to MCP23008 based type and Address 32 (0x20).

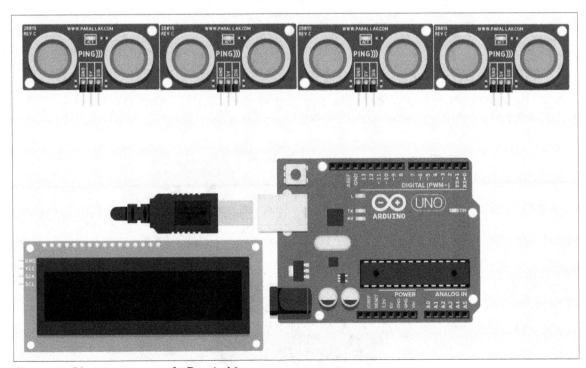

Figure-90. Placing components for Practical 3

- Connect the **Power** terminals of all four sensors and similarly, connect the **Ground** terminals of all four sensors; refer to Figure-91.

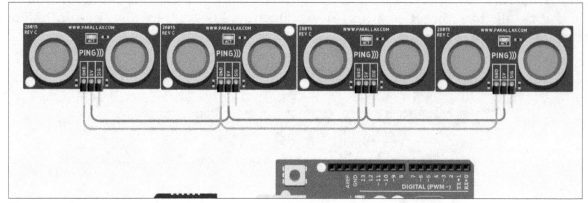

Figure-91. Connecting pins of sensors

- Connect the **Power** and **Ground** pins of right-most Ultra Sonic Distance sensor to 5V and GND POWER pins of Arduino; refer to Figure-92.

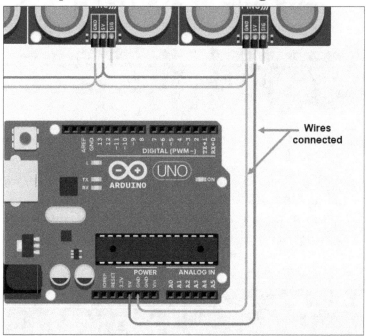

Figure-92. Providing power to sensors

- Similarly, connect GND and VCC pins of LCD to GND and 5V pins of left-most Ultra Sonic Distance sensor; refer to Figure-93.

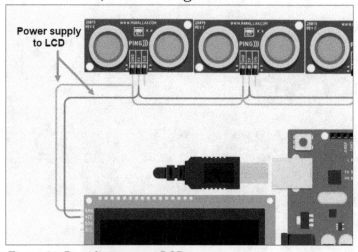

Figure-93. Providing power to LCD

- Connect the SDA and SCL pins of LCD to same pins on Arduino; refer to Figure-94.

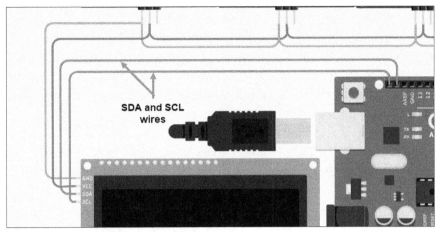

Figure-94. Connecting SDA and SCL wires

- Click on the **Notes** tool and place note on first ultra sonic distance sensor from left, and type its name Front sensor. Similarly, apply names to other sensors in sequence as Back Sensor, Left Sensor, and Right Sensor.

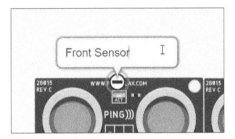

Figure-95. Adding note to sensor

- Connect SIG pin of Front sensor to Digital Pin 13 of Arduino, SIG pin of Back sensor to Digital Pin 12 of Arduino, SIG pin of Left sensor to Digital Pin 11 of Arduino, SIG pin of Right sensor to Digital Pin 10 of Arduino; refer to Figure-96.

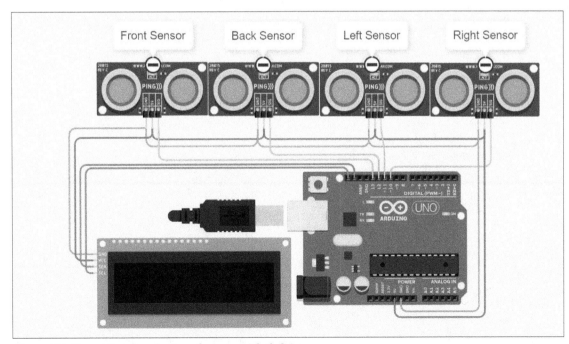

Figure-96. Connecting signal wires of sensors with Arduino

- This completes the full circuit. Now, we will use blocks for coding.

For programming this circuit, we will use input from Ultra sonic distance sensor at pin number 13 of Arduino and compare it with value 45 cms. If the value of distance provided by sensor is less than 45 then message will be printed on LCD screen. We will create code blocks for one sensor and copy-paste it for other sensors. Later we will change the pin numbers and LCD messages for these sensor code blocks. The procedure is given next.

- Click on the **Code** button from toolbar and select **Control** button from the **Blocks** panel. List of available code blocks will be displayed; refer to Figure-97.

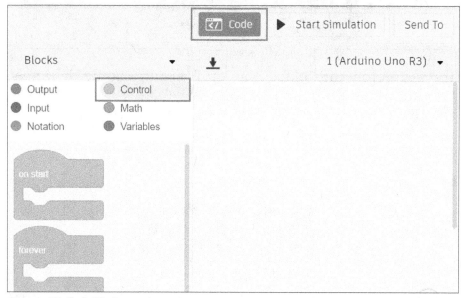

Figure-97. Code Blocks panel

- Scroll down in the panel and drag the **if-then** block in **forever** block of programming area; refer to Figure-98.

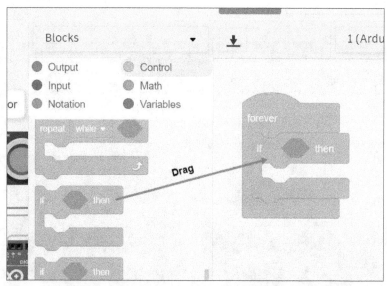

Figure-98. Placing if-then block

- Now insert **Comparison** block from **Math** library in empty slot of **if** block in the programming area; refer to Figure-99.

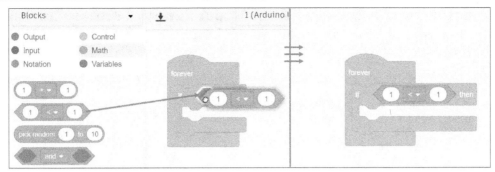

Figure-99. Inserting comparison block

- Drag the **read ultrasonic distance sensor on trigger pin** block from **Input** library of **Blocks** panel to value input box of **Comparison** block recently placed; refer to Figure-100.

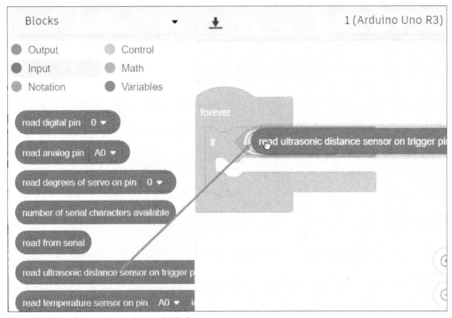

Figure-100. Placing sensor read block

- Set the pin number to **13**, units to **cm**, and echo pin to **same as trigger** in read block recently placed and type the value as **45** in other input box of comparison block; refer to Figure-101.

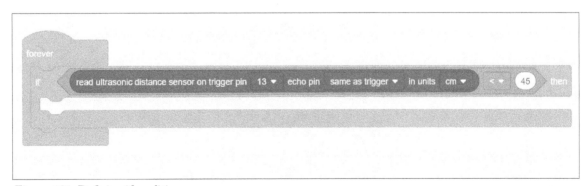

Figure-101. Defining if condition

- Drag the **print to LCD** code block from **Output** library of **Blocks** panel and place it in empty then slot of **if** block earlier placed. Set the output text to **"Check Front"**; refer to Figure-102.

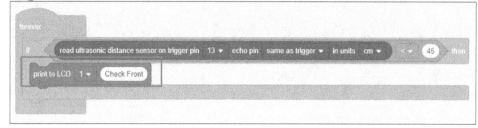

Figure-102. Defining text to be shown on LCD

- Since, we adding four sensors and it might happen that all four sensors start to give message. In such case, there should be some delay between showing consecutive messages on LCD because there is limited display area on LCD and between these delays you need to clear the screen to prepare LCD for next message. So, now we will add **wait** block and **on LCD clear the screen** blocks from **Control** and **Output** libraries of **Blocks** panel, respectively; refer to Figure-103. We have specified delay as 200 milliseconds to shorten the refresh rate of LCD.

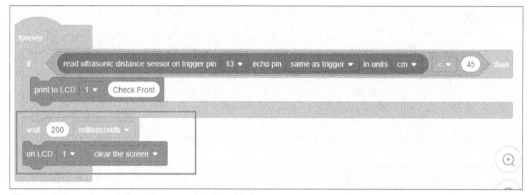

Figure-103. wait and clear the screen blocks added

- Right-click on **If-then** block earlier placed and select **Duplicate** option from shortcut menu; refer to Figure-104. The duplicate copy of **If-then**, **wait**, and **on LCD clear the screen** blocks will get attached to cursor.

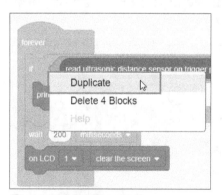

Figure-104. Duplicate option

- Place the duplicate copy below the **on LCD clear the screen** block of **forever** block; refer to Figure-105.

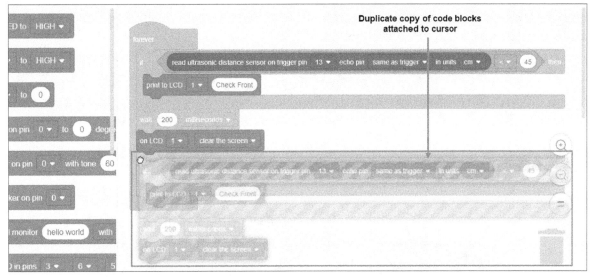

Figure-105. Duplicating blocks

- Right-click again on the previous **If-then** block and select **Duplicate** option from the shortcut menu. Duplicate copy of both block sets will be created and get attached to cursor.
- Place them below the previous code blocks in the **forever** block.
- Now, match the pin numbers and LCD messages as shown in Figure-106. This completes the programming of circuit. Click on the **Code** button again to hide **Programming** panel.

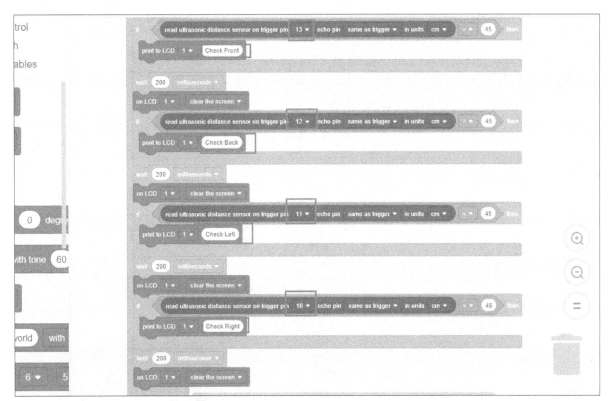

Figure-106. Matching pins and messages

To start the simulation, click on the **Start Simulation** button from the toolbar and move the distance points of sensors to check results on LCD.

If you have understanding of Code blocks programming then its a good challenge to modify this code to show "**All Safe**" when each sensor is giving reading of more than **45** centimeters.

PRACTICE 1

Create a circuit to read range of output value generated at digital pin by Flex sensor as shown in Figure-107. This range should be displayed in the Serial Monitor.

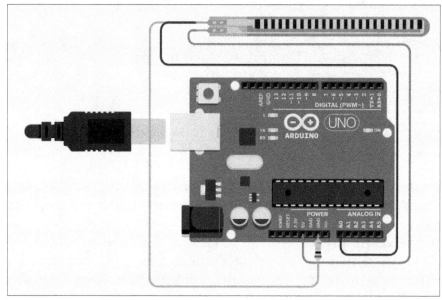

Figure-107. Practice drawing for circuit

Check next page for code blocks, if needed.

PRACTICE 2

Create a circuit using ATTINY chip that changes color of LED based on flexing degree of Flex sensor as shown in Figure-108.

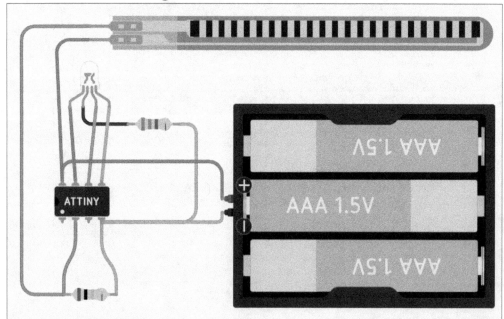

Figure-108. Practice 2 circuit

Check next page for code blocks if needed.

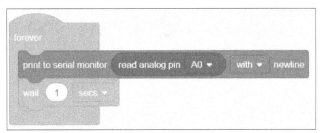

Figure-109. Practice 1 code block

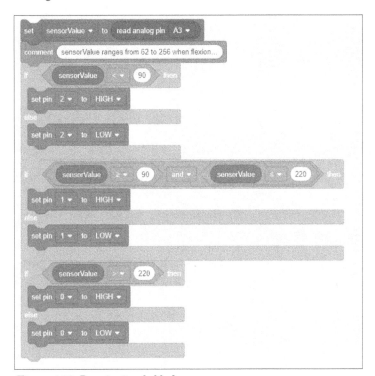

Figure-110. Practice 2 code blocks

FOR STUDENT NOTES

Chapter 4

Basics of Programming Code

Topics Covered

The major topics covered in this chapter are:

- *Basics of C++ Programming for Arduino and ATTINY*
- *Using AI tools like ChatGPT for programming*

WHY PROGRAMMING

In previous chapter, you have learned to create different types of circuits and use blocks for programming. When working with programmable devices like Arduino, ATTINY, and Micro:bit; you will find that there are many attachable components for which block codes are not available in Tinkercad. For example, you cannot program Neopixel LEDs using Block program (at least till writing this book). For that, you will be depending on writing text codes of program to perform operations. You will be using programming languages like C++, Java, Python, and so on. In this chapter, we will use C++ as base for delivering information. You can apply same concepts to other languages as well when need in your project. Note that motive of this chapter is to provide you basics of C++ so that you can understand and perform simple tweaks when using programs generated by AI tools. We will not get our hands dirty in programming everything when we can use AI tools to generate program codes because that is what they do best.

INTRODUCTION TO C++ FOR NON-PROGRAMMERS

Programming language is a way to tell your computer, what is to be done. Just like we use words to speak our language, computers use programming language keywords and variables to understand what we want them to do. Here, Keywords are commands and variables are parameters. For example, if I say "Lift this box to 5 feet height"; then "Lift" is a command (keyword) and "5 feet height" is variable.

Variables and Variable Types

Variables are values that we use in programming. You have earlier created number variables in Code block programming and Circuit Designs in previous chapters. The number variable that you created in previous chapters is called **integer** which can store values without decimal. There are many other types of variables that can be created in C++. These variables can store text, character, number with decimal point, numbers in fraction, and true/false values. Various types of variables available in C++ are given next.

If asked why you should learn about variables then it is important because if you want to display your name in LCD display using Arduino and programming language then you should know that the value can be stored in string and not in integer.

Integer

The integer variable is used to store whole numbers starting from -2,147,483,648 to 2,147,483,647. There are two types of integers, signed and unsigned. Signed integers can store and display negative values as well as positive values whereas unsigned integers will be able to store and display only positive values. These variables are defined as

int a = 2;

In this code line, int is keyword used to define that "**a**" is an integer variable which has initial value as **2**. So, in my program I can use "**a**" in place of **2** value whenever required. Note that at the end of each program code, you need to type "**;**" to mark end of the code line. Keep in mind that now "**a**" is an integer type of container. Later, I can put **5** in place of **2** in "**a**" if needed and then it will act as **5** in the program.

Float

Float is used to store values that are with decimal point. For example 142.2523, 34.12, and so on. You can store 7 digits in float variable including the decimal point. The variable is defined as:

float a = 234.3453;

In this code, float is keyword used to define "**a**" variable as float type which can store values with decimal point.

Double

Double is used to store value with decimal point similar to float but it can store larger numbers with 16 digits including decimal point. The procedure to define double variable is same as :

double a = 56165.8461684;

Character

A character is an alphabet or ASCII symbol that can be stored. For example, d, t, s, @, %, and so on. The variable is defined as:

char a = '$';

Note that it is important to close the character in single quotes (' ') when defining.

String

A string is a series of characters arranged in linear order. The variable is defined as:

string a = "CADCAMCAE Works";

Note that it is important to close the string in double quotes (" ") when defining.

Boolean

A boolean is a type of variable that can store True or False value. The variable is defined as:

bool a = true;
bool b = false;

Variable Modifiers

Variable modifiers are used to increase/decrease the size of basic data types. There are mainly four variable modifiers; signed, unsigned, short, long, and const. The codes to use these modifiers are given next.

signed int a = -15;

This will store value -15 in integer variable a.

Unsigned int a = 50;

This will store value 50 in integer without any sign. Note that if you try to assign a negative value to unsigned integer then system will subtract that value from

4,294,967,296 and show you the result. So, if you try to save -50 in unsigned integer then it will store 4,294,967,296 - 50 = 4,294,967,246

short int a = 5465;

This variable can store 4 to 5 digits.

long int a = 548916846446546178;

This variable can store 18 to 19 digits.

const int a =34;

This code means value of integer a will remain 34 and it cannot be changed by program.

Auto

auto keyword is used to automatically define type of variable based on value specified for it. For example, the below code will automatically create **s** as integer type.

auto s = 564;

Arrays

Array is a collection of multiple variables in a single variable. You can consider it as a large tub in which multiple small containers can fit. If you are familiar with Matrix of mathematics then arrays are matrix that can be NxN type. You can create single column array or you can create 3 dimensional arrays. The method to define an array is given next.

```
int a [4] = {1,2,3,4};
int b[3][4] = {
                {1, 2, 3, 4},
                {5, 6, 7, 8},
                {9, 10, 11, 12}
                };
```

In this case, if you want to access second variable of **a** array then you will use a[1] which will give output 2. Note that address values of arrays start from 0, so a[4] array will have a[0], a[1], a[2], a[3] variables. Two dimensional array b[3][4] has three rows and 4 columns. To access value of variable in 2nd row and 3rd column of this array, you will use b[1][2] as variable.

Pointers

Pointers are generally associated with arrays but you can use them with any variable. Pointer is used to store address value of a variable. Address is the location in your storage device (hard drive) where variable value is stored. The method is given next.

```
int a = 10;
int *ptr = &a;
```

In first line of this code, we have created a variable with a value of 10. In next line, we have created an integer pointer **ptr** that stores the address of **a**. When we place **&** before variable's name then it shows address of the variable, not the value. When we place ***** before variable's name then it marks the variable as pointer.

Reference

References are used to provide multiple names to same address value. This is done to make code easy to understand in reference to current running function. You will learn about function later in this chapter. The method to create reference variable is given next.

int a = 15;
int &b = a;

In this code, we have created **a** variable with value **15** and then we have created reference variable **b** which refers to the value of **a**. Creating this code means **a** and **b** both are using same address in storage device so they are pointing to same value **15** at this time. If we make **b = 10**; in code then **a** will also become **10**.

User Defined Variables

There are three types of user defined variables that can be created in C++; Enumerator, Structure, and Class. These types are discussed next.

Enumerator

Enumerator is created by keyword enum. It is used to generate a variable that contains set of multiple values. Assume that you want to create a variable color which has 3 colors Red, Green, and Blue in it. Depending on your requirement in programming, you want to use all three colors of set or just one color. Now, scale up this example of 200 values and think how many declarations will be required if enum keyword has not existed. The method to create enumerator variable is given next.

enum x {Red, Green, Blue};
x clr = Green;

In this code, **x** is declared as enumerator which can have values Red, Green, and Blue. Note that there is no = sign when declaring enumerator. In next line, we define **clr** as variable of type **x** and make it equal to Green. So, our new variable **clr** has value Green stored in it. Note that at deeper level values defined under enum x are just named integers where Red is 0, Green is 1, and Blue is 2; but we will not be using that information in our course.

Structure

Structure is collection of variables with different types. You can create a structure which has two integer, two character, and one boolean type variables. The method to create structure variable is given next.

```
struct a {
        int x = 10; int y = 20; char ab = 'm' ; char bc = 'n'; bool tr = true;
        };
```

```
a mystr = {12,13,r,s,false};
```

In this code, you have created a structure variable named **a** which has two integer variables **x** and **y**, two character variables, **ab** and **bc**, and one boolean variable **tr**. In next code, you have created variable **mystr** which is structure variable of type **a** also you have assigned new values to variables of structure. Now, if you want to use value of second integer of **mystr** variable then you will use **mystr.y**. Similarly, if you want to use value of boolean variable of structure then you will use **mystr.tr**.

Class

Class is used when you want to create a type of variable that includes functions along with variables. Functions are used to perform actions in programming language. You will learn about functions later. The method to create a class variable is given next.

```
class motion {
            int position [3] = {0,0,0};
            void rotate()
            {
            angle = angle + 10;
            }
        };
motion m1;
```

In this code, we have created a class variable **m1** which has all the functions and variables of motion class included in it. The variables created using class are called objects of class. So, if you want to use function rotate of this class then you will use **m1.rotate()** and if you want to use position variable then you will type **m1.position**.

Changing Variable Type

Changing a variable from one type to another type is called type casting. This is performed to keep the memory usage of program to minimal. The code to perform type casting are given next.

```
int x = 5;
float y = static cast<float>(x);
```

In this code, although **x** was declared integer but as second line is compiled by program then it becomes equivalent to **y** which is a float so **x** also become a float variable.

There is also a dynamic cast syntax used for changing type of class variables but that is not our scope of work here.

Functions

Functions are the sections of program code which perform action. For example, you can create functions to add and subtract values, move objects, rotate wheels, and so on. Functions are also used to control your Arduino board operation which is the purpose of this chapter. An example of codes for creating function is given next.

```
int multiply (int a, int b)
{
int c = a*b;
return c;
};
```

In this code, we have created function **multiply** which takes two integer input **a** and **b**. After performing calculations using values of **a** and **b**, the function returns an integer value **c**. Note that **int** written before function name defines what type of value will be returned by this function. If we had written **char multiply (int a, int b)** then its return (output) value would have been a character.

Similarly, when you will be working on creating program to run LEDs of Neopixel or LCDs then you will be using such functions. For example, below function defines which pins of LCD are to be used for output.

```
LiquidCrystal lcd(7, 8, 12, 11, 10, 9);
```

This is a function of LiquidCrystal.h library. You will learn about libraries in this chapter.

Non-Return Functions

If you add void before the name of function instead of variable then your function does not return anything as variable which can be used by other functions. In this case, you will not write return in the function definition as demonstrated next.

```
void birthdaywish(string s)
{
cout<<"Happy Birthday", <<s;
};
```

The function **birthdaywish** does not return any variable, although it will print **Happy Birthday** and whatever is written for **s** when using this function. So, when you will be using this function in coding, you will write **birthdaywish("My Friend");** and computer will print **Happy Birthday My Friend**. In this function, we have used **cout** keyword. This **cout** keyword is used to print/display strings and variables. You will learn about more such keywords.

Similarly, a function can be non-argument taking function. In such case, there is no need to write anything inside the () when creating function. Like,

```
void birthdaywish()
{
cout<<"Happy Birthday";
};
```

Scope of Variables

Variables created in C++ programs have their boundaries out of which they are not known. A variable created inside one function will not be known to another function unless it is created as global variable. So, variables created inside a function are local variables and variables created outside of all the functions in C++ program are global variables.

It means we can use same variable names a, b, and c in different functions and inside each function they will hold their own unique values and addresses. If we want to use same variable with same value and same address then we will create it outside all the functions. The codes given next are an example of variable scope.

```
int x = 10;

int div (int a)
{
int c = x/a;
return c;
};
int y=a;        //this is wrong
```

In this code, **x** is declared outside of functions, so you can use it inside function for calculation but **a** variable is declared inside the function, so you cannot use it outside of this div function.

Preprocessors

Preprocessors are created using # before their names in C and C++ languages. The preprocessors are used when you want to declare or add something before the system starts to run the program. In our case of programming Arduino and other boards, these preprocessors are used to define alternative names for numbers. For example, **#define LED 6** will allow us to use LED in place of 6 wherever need in program. You can even get the output of **LED+5** as **11**. Various preprocessors are given in next table with their purpose.

Preprocessor Directives	Description
#define	Used to define a macro.
#undef	Used to undefine a macro.
#include	Used to include a file in the source code program.
#ifdef	Used to include a section of code if a certain macro is defined by #define.
#ifndef	Used to include a section of code if a certain macro is not defined by #define.
#if	Check for the specified condition.
#else	Alternate code that executes when #if fails.
#endif	Used to mark the end of #if, #ifdef, and #ifndef.
#error	Used to generate a compilation error message.

#line	Used to modify line number and filename information.
#pragma once	To make sure the header is included only once.
#pragma message	Used for displaying a message during compilation.

Header Files

Header files are libraries provided by hardware manufacturers, software developers, and open source community. These libraries contain 10s to 1000s of functions that can be used directly with the help of understanding the documentation of header file. For example, I want to use Neopixel LEDs and I know that Adafruit NeoPixel.h is a header file that contains functions related to the use of these LEDs. Then, at the beginning of program, I will add:

#include <Adafruit NeoPixel.h>

Note that there is no ; at the end of this statement. Now, I will look for documentation of Adafruit NeoPixel.h library on internet. One such place where I can find documentation of this library will be **https://github.com/adafruit/Adafruit NeoPixel**. Click on the Read Me file and examples on this page to learn about input and output of various functions of this library and how you can utilize them in your Tinkercad circuit projects.

Once you have added code #include <Adafruit NeoPixel.h> then you will create a new class variable so that you can use functions of Adafruit NeoPixel.h library as given next.

Adafruit NeoPixel abc = Adafruit NeoPixel(NUMPIXELS, LED, NEO GRB + NEO KHZ800);

Here, abc is a new class element which has all the functions which were available in Adafruit NeoPixel.h library. So, if you want to use setbrightness function of the library then you will use the statement:

abc.setbrightness(120);

Keywords of C++ and Their usage

The list of keywords mostly used in programming with C++ is given next. Refer to QR code at the end of this table to learn more about C++ keywords and other concepts of programming because here we have just touched the surface of C++.

Keyword	Description
and	An alternative way to write the logical && operator
and eq	An alternative way to write the &= assignment operator
bitand	An alternative way to write the & bitwise operator
bitor	An alternative way to write the | bitwise operator
bool	A data type that can only store true or false values
break	Breaks out of a loop or a switch block

case	Marks a block of code in switch statements
catch	Catches exceptions generated by try statements
char	A data type that can store a single character
class	Defines a class
compl	An alternative way to write the ~ bitwise operator
const	Defines a variable or parameter as a constant (unchangeable) or specifies that a class method does not modify attributes of the class
continue	Continues to the next iteration of a loop
default	Specifies the default block of code in a switch statement
delete	Makes dynamic memory free for allocation
do	Used together with while to create a do/while loop
double	A data type that is usually 64 bits long which can store fractional numbers
else	Used in conditional statements
enum	Declares an enumerated type
FALSE	A boolean value equivalent to 0
float	A data type that is usually 32 bits long which can store fractional numbers
for	Creates a for loop
friend	Specifies classes and functions which have access to private and protected members
goto	Jumps to a line of code specified by a label
if	Makes a conditional statement
int	A data type that is usually 32 bits long which can store whole numbers
long	Ensures that an integer is at least 32 bits long (use long to ensure 64 bits)
namespace	Declares a namespace
new	Reserves dynamic memory
not	An alternative way to write the logical ! operator
not eq	An alternative way to write the != comparison operator
or	An alternative way to write the logical || operator
or eq	An alternative way to write the |= assignment operator
private	An access modifier which makes a member only accessible within the declared class
protected	An access modifier which makes a member only accessible within the declared class and its children
public	An access modifier which makes a member accessible from anywhere
return	Used to return a value from a function
short	Reduces the size of an integer to 16 bits
signed	Specifies that an int or char can represent positive and negative values (this is the default so the keyword is not usually necessary)

sizeof	An operator that returns the amount of memory occupied by a variable or data type
static	Specifies that an attribute or method belongs to the class itself instead of instances of the class
	Specifies that a variable in a function keeps its value after the function ends
struct	Defines a structure
switch	Selects one of many code blocks to be executed
template	Declares a template class or template function
this	A variable that is available inside class methods and constructors which contains a pointer to a class instance
throw	Creates a custom error which can be caught by a try...catch statement
TRUE	A boolean value equivalent to 1
try	Creates a try...catch statement
typedef	Defines a custom data type
unsigned	Specifies that an int or char should only represent positive values which allows for storing numbers up to twice as large
using	Allows variables and functions from a namespace to be used without the namespace's prefix
virtual	Specifies that a class method is virtual
void	Indicates a function that does not return a value or specifies a pointer to a data with an unspecified type
while	Creates a while loop
xor	An alternative way to write the ^ bitwise operator
xor eq	An alternative way to write the ^= assignment operator

https://www.w3schools.com/cpp/default.asp

C++ Programming Tutorials

USING AI TOOLS FOR PROGRAMMING ARDUINO AND OTHER PROGRAMMABLE DEVICES

In recent time, AI tools like ChatGPT, Gemini, Copilot, ARIA, and so on have become very popular and for the right reason as they have made it easy for common folks like us to use some basic programs to get by. All these tools use NLP (Natural Language Processing) model which allows us to send instructions to computer using our own language like text written in this book. For example, If I write "Give me a stunning image of Taj Mahal in evening with green moon" to ARIA tool of Opera browser then it will generate an image. Although, it is not possible to get Moon to be green unless something phenomenal happens but still, these AI tools are able to understand our natural language and create something that cannot exist. This computer power of AI shine bright when we ask it to generate basic programs in various programming languages like C++. Getting back to our topic, we have created a circuit of Arduino, PIR sensor, and NeoPixel Ring 12 as shown in Figure-1.

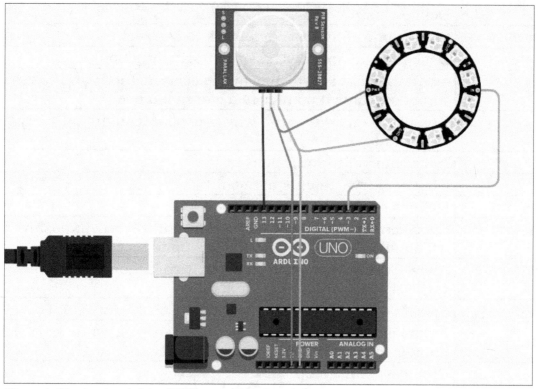

Figure-1. Circuit using Arduino PIR Sensor and NeoPixel LEDs

In this circuit, we have connected 5V and Ground pins of Arduino to both PIR sensor and NeoPixel Ring 12. We have connected Digital pin 13 of Arduino to Signal pin of PIR sensor. We have connected In pin of NeoPixel Ring 12 to Pin 3 of Arduino.

Suppose, we want that color of this NeoPixel ring should change whenever motion is detected by the PIR sensor. We can generate the programming codes by copy pasting the above paragraph with one added prompt "Write a program for me in which color of neopixel changes randomly when motion is detected by PIR sensor otherwise it remains unchanged." So, our prompt to type in ChatGPT or any other AI tool becomes:

In Tinkercad circuits, I have connected 5V and ground to both PIR sensor and NeoPixel Ring 12. I have connected Digital pin 13 of Arduino to Signal pin of PIR sensor. I have connected Digital Pin 3 of Arduino to In pin of NeoPixel Ring 12. Write a program for me in which color of neopixel changes randomly when motion is detected by PIR sensor otherwise it remains unchanged.

After running this prompt, AI will create a program; refer to Figure-2.

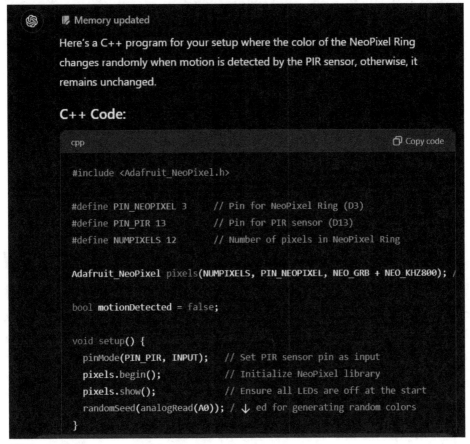

Figure-2. Program generated by chatgpt

You need to copy this program from AI chat window and paste it in **Code** panel of the **Tinkercad Circuits** application; refer to Figure-3. Note that you need to delete everything that was in **Code** panel before pasting the new codes.

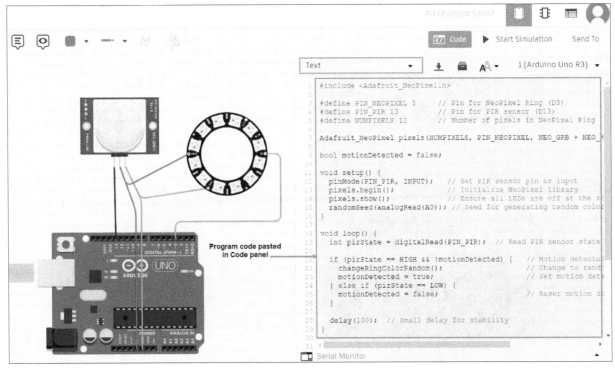

Figure-3. Copy pasting codes

You can now simulate the circuit and check the output by moving PIR sensor detection point; refer to Figure-4.

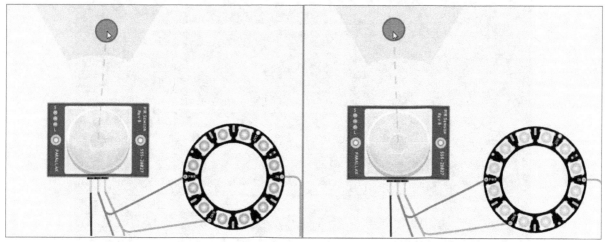

Figure-4. Simulating circuit

Similarly, you can generate programs for other programmable devices like Micro:bit and ATTINY. Note that you need to be sure about the input and output capabilities of pins on your programmable devices to which you are connecting the sensors and output devices. Also, you should check the program comments generated by AI to understand whether program is doing what you want it to do.

PRACTICAL

Create a copy of the Circuit earlier created in Practical 3 of Chapter 3; refer to Figure-5 and reprogram it so that distance of sensors is displayed with initial letter for each sensor. For example, if distance from Front sensor is 80 cm, from Back sensor is 60 cm, from Left sensor is 40 cm, and from Right sensor is 100 cm then it will display `F80 B60 L40 R100` in LCD screen.

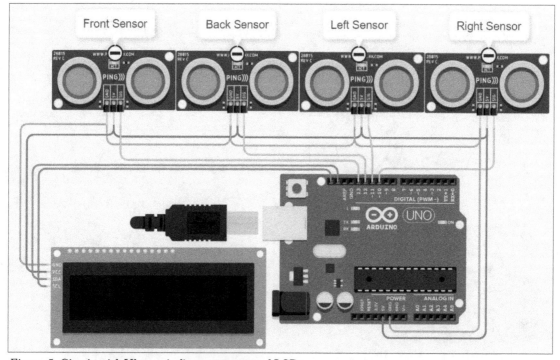

Figure-5. Circuit with Ultrasonic distance sensors and LCD

Creating Prompt for AI

- First, we will collect the information about what are the components in our circuit. So, in this circuit **I have four Ultrasonic Distance Sensors, one LCD 16x2 (I2C), and one Arduino Uno R3**.

- Next, we will describe connections done in our circuit. So, in this circuit **I have connected power to all four ultrasonic distance sensors and LCD from 5V and GND POWER pins of Arduino. I have connected SIG pin of Front ultrasonic sensor with Digital Pin 13 of Arduino, SIG pin of Back ultrasonic sensor with Digital Pin 12 of Arduino, SIG pin of Left ultrasonic sensor with Digital Pin 11 of Arduino and SIG pin of Right ultrasonic sensor with Digital Pin 10 of Arduino. SDA and SCL pins of LCD are connected to SDA and SCL pins of Arduino.**

- Now, we will provide the directions on what we want to perform by using programming codes. So, we will write: **Create a program for Tinkercad circuit in which distance detected by Front ultrasonic sensor is displayed with F prefix in LCD then there is space of one letter after that distance detected by Back ultrasonic sensor is displayed with B prefix in LCD then there is one letter space after that distance detected by Left ultrasonic sensor is displayed with L prefix in LCD then there is one letter space after that distance detected by Right ultrasonic sensor is displayed with R prefix in LCD.**

- Now, add these three prompts together and feed it to any AI tool. You will get program output which will use two libraries <Wire.h> and <LiquidCrystal I2C.h> but when you run that program in Tinkercad Circuit, the program will generate errors. In this case, with little search on internet, you will be able to find that for using LCD 16x2 (I2C) in Tinkercad, you will need <Adafruit LiquidCrystal.h> library instead of <LiquidCrystal I2C.h>. So, we will add one more line in our prompt: **Use Adafruit LiquidCrystal.h library**. We are using Ultrasonic distance sensors which have same pin for trigger and echo so, we will explicitly tell AI to use same pin by using prompt: **My ultrasonic sensors have same pin for trigger and echo.** It may be possible that program tries to display all the text in single row on LCD which will not fit the screen. So, we can add the prompt: **Display sensor reading text in two rows in LCD with Front and Back readings in first row and Left and Right readings in second row.** Combine all the prompts written in bold in this text and you will get your final prompt based on which final program will be generated.

Simulating Sensors

- Feed the prompt generated by combining all the prompts earlier discussed to ChatGPT or other AI tool. The program will be generated with important comments like at what address should be the LCD.

- Copy-paste the codes in **Text** field of **Code** panel in Tinkercad and simulate to check function; refer to Figure-6.

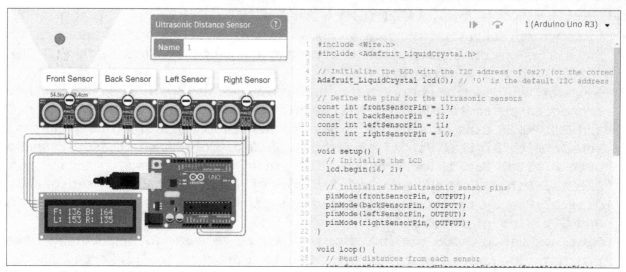

Figure-6. Final simulation of circuit

This line ends the final chapter of this book but mark it as beginning line for your imagination with electronics and programmable devices. After you become comfortable with working on Arduino, there is a lot more to explore like PLCs, evaluation boards from manufacturers like Infineon, ECU in cars, LED TVs, and so on.

Index

OTHER BOOKS BY CADCAMCAE WORKS

Autodesk Revit 2025 Black Book
Autodesk Revit 2024 Black Book
Autodesk Revit 2023 Black Book
Autodesk Revit 2022 Black Book
Autodesk Revit 2021 Black Book

Autodesk Inventor 2025 Black Book
Autodesk Inventor 2024 Black Book
Autodesk Inventor 2023 Black Book
Autodesk Inventor 2022 Black Book
Autodesk Inventor 2021 Black Book

Autodesk Fusion 360 Black Book (V 2.0.18477)

Autodesk Fusion 360 PCB Black Book (V 2.0.18719)

AutoCAD Electrical 2025 Black Book
AutoCAD Electrical 2024 Black Book
AutoCAD Electrical 2023 Black Book
AutoCAD Electrical 2022 Black Book
AutoCAD Electrical 2021 Black Book

SolidWorks 2024 Black Book
SolidWorks 2023 Black Book
SolidWorks 2022 Black Book

SolidWorks Simulation 2024 Black Book
SolidWorks Simulation 2023 Black Book
SolidWorks Simulation 2022 Black Book

SolidWorks Flow Simulation 2024 Black Book
SolidWorks Flow Simulation 2023 Black Book
SolidWorks Flow Simulation 2022 Black Book

SolidWorks CAM 2024 Black Book
SolidWorks CAM 2023 Black Book
SolidWorks CAM 2022 Black Book

SolidWorks Electrical 2024 Black Book
SolidWorks Electrical 2023 Black Book
SolidWorks Electrical 2022 Black Book

SolidWorks Workbook 2022

Mastercam 2023 for SolidWorks Black Book
Mastercam 2022 for SolidWorks Black Book
Mastercam 2017 for SolidWorks Black Book

Mastercam 2025 Black Book
Mastercam 2024 Black Book
Mastercam 2023 Black Book
Mastercam 2022 Black Book

Creo Parametric 11.0 Black Book
Creo Parametric 10.0 Black Book
Creo Parametric 9.0 Black Book
Creo Parametric 8.0 Black Book

Creo Manufacturing 11.0 Black Book
Creo Manufacturing 10.0 Black Book
Creo Manufacturing 9.0 Black Book

ETABS V21 Black Book
ETABS V20 Black Book
ETABS V19 Black Book

Basics of Autodesk Inventor Nastran 2025
Basics of Autodesk Inventor Nastran 2024
Basics of Autodesk Inventor Nastran 2022

Autodesk CFD 2024 Black Book
Autodesk CFD 2023 Black Book
Autodesk CFD 2021 Black Book

FreeCAD 0.21 Black Book
FreeCAD 0.20 Black Book
FreeCAD 0.19 Black Book

Page Left Blank Intentionally